ROO ON THE ROCK

Mandy crouched with Katie beside the injured roo. 'That driver never even stopped to see if she was still alive!' she whispered, feeling tears sting her eyelids.

As they moved off, the kangaroo made a feeble attempt to lift her head. She struggled and gave up.

'What is it? What do you want?' Mandy turned and took a last look out of the back window at the scene of the accident. Up on the rock, the shadowy roos called out. 'Wait!' she cried.

A young kangaroo about the size of a small dog had crept out of the ditch.

The injured roo lifted her head, too weak to call out.

'It's her joey! She's a mother and that's her baby!'

Animal Ark series

1 Kittens in the Kitchen
2 Pony in the Porch
3 Puppies in the Pantry
4 Goat in the Garden
5 Hedgehogs in the Hall
6 Badger in the Basement
7 Cub in the Cupboard
8 Piglet in a Playpen
9 Owl in the Office
10 Lamb in the Laundry
11 Bunnies in the Bathroom
12 Donkey on the Doorstep
13 Hamster in a Hamper
14 Goose on the Loose
15 Calf in the Cottage
16 Koalas in a Crisis
17 Wombat in the Wild
18 Roo on the Rock
19 Squirrels in the School
20 Guinea-pig in the Garage
21 Fawn in the Forest
22 Shetland in the Shed
23 Swan in the Swim
24 Lion by the Lake
25 Elephants in the East
26 Monkeys on the Mountain
27 Dog at the Door
28 Foals in the Field
29 Sheep at the Show
30 Racoons on the Roof
31 Dolphin in the Deep
32 Bears in the Barn
33 Otter in the Outhouse
34 Whale in the Waves
35 Hound at the Hospital

36 Rabbits on the Run
37 Horse in the House
38 Panda in the Park
39 Tiger on the Track
40 Gorilla in the Glade
41 Tabby in the Tub
42 Chinchilla up the Chimney
43 Puppy in a Puddle
44 Leopard at the Lodge
45 Giraffe in a Jam
46 Hippo in a Hole
47 Foxes on the Farm
48 Badgers by the Bridge
49 Deer on the Drive
50 Animals in the Ark
51 Mare in the Meadow
52 Cats in the Caravan
Hauntings 1: Dog in the Dungeon
Hauntings 2: Cat in the Crypt
Hauntings 3: Stallion in the Storm
Hauntings 4: Wolf at the Window
Hauntings 5: Hound on the Heath
Hauntings 6: Colt in the Cave
Ponies at the Point
Seal on the Shore
Pigs at the Picnic
Sheepdog in the Snow
Kitten in the Cold
Fox in the Frost
Hamster in the Holly
Pony in the Post
Pup at the Palace
Mouse in the Mistletoe
Animal Ark Favourites
Wildlife Ways

LUCY DANIELS

Roo
– on the –
Rock

Illustrated by Shelagh McNicholas

Hodder
Children's
Books

a division of Hodder Headline Limited

Special thanks to Jenny Oldfield.
Thanks also to veterinarian Bairbre O'Malley for reviewing the
information contained in this book.

Winnie the Pooh by A. A. Milne
published by Methuen Children's Books 1926
by permission of Reed Books

Animal Ark is a trademark of Working Partners Ltd
Text copyright © 1996 Working Partners Ltd
Created by Working Partners Ltd, London W6 0QT
Original series created by Ben M. Baglio

First published in Great Britain in 1996
by Hodder Children's Books

A Catalogue record for this book is available from the British Library.

ISBN 0 340 65581 X

Typeset by Avon Dataset Ltd, Bidford-on-Avon, Warks

Printed and bound in Great Britain by
Clays Ltd, St Ives plc

Hodder Children's Books
a division of Hodder Headline Limited
338 Euston Road
London NW1 3BH

One

Mandy Hope sat listening to Katie Browne who was whistling as she drove. She yawned, wishing that the journey was over. The red sun was low in the sky. It was late in a hot March day at the end of a long, dry Australian summer.

Katie swerved to avoid a gang of little hare wallabies that ran like the wind along the side of the rough road. Heads up, forelegs dangling, they seemed to be whistling back at her.

Mandy sat in the back of the powerful Landcruiser with her friend, Gary Simpson. They watched the wallabies dash ahead, then dart back on their tracks, disappearing into the bush as fast as they'd come. Mandy held her breath. The beautiful creatures, with their large, pointed ears and dark eyes, seemed to be running straight into danger.

'You Aussies are only twenty-five million years behind the times!' Adam Hope wisecracked at Katie, the nurse at Mitchell Gap Veterinary Centre.

Katie slowed down to take a bend and began to climb the hill that would take them through the small town of Mitchell to Mandy's home, the vets' practice at Mitchell Gap which was run by her mother and father. 'So how come, according to you we're past our sell-by date?' Katie challenged Mandy's dad.

Half-dozing in the back of the car, Mandy grinned as she listened to their nurse stand up to him.

'Because!' He waved his arms at the mountainous countryside. 'For a start, the sea cut you off from the rest of the world at least sixty million years ago. And secondly, you have over a hundred species of that strange type of mammal, the marsupial!' He put on a jokey voice; a kind of studious, know-it-all tone.

'Ignore him!' Mandy whispered to Gary. She

shifted to get comfortable. They'd been driving all day, home from Melbourne Zoo. Katie had organised the four-day trip to give them close-up views of koalas and flying squirrels, emus, black swans and lyre birds, together with funnel-web spiders, crocodiles and snakes. Mandy had loved every minute; especially the nursery section which housed the orphan joeys and wallabies. But now she would be glad to get home to their house by the freshwater creek, with its shady veranda and cool swimming-pool. In fact, she could hardly wait.

'So?' Katie took another bend. The wallabies reappeared out of nowhere and raced alongside.

Mandy flinched and looked the other way.

'So, in Europe and North America, marsupials have been extinct for twenty-five million years!' Mr Hope declared. 'Like I said, you're behind the times. Where else would you find over a hundred species of animals that still tuck their babies into a pocket and lug them round with them wherever they go?'

Mandy saw the wallabies veer off again. She relaxed and rested her head back against the seat. 'I think that's neat! Ready-made pockets!' she grinned. She loved the way Nature solved problems like how to carry your young.

Her dad turned with a wink. 'You would! Whose side are you on?'

'Katie's.'

'Traitor! Take the kookaburra, for instance.' Mr Hope went on.

'A kookaburra isn't a marsupial,' Mandy pointed out. 'It's a bird!'

'I know that. I'm just using it as another example of the crazy animals over here. Here you have a kingfisher which can't fish. So what does he do? He eats rats and reptiles instead!'

'We *like* kookaburras, don't we, Katie?' Mandy had grown used to the bird's weird cry during her five months in Australia. One woke them each morning, calling from the acacia tree behind the house.

'It sounds like a donkey laughing,' her dad complained. 'I can't get my beauty sleep because of that jackass racket!'

'Not for much longer,' Gary reminded him. The trip to Melbourne Zoo had been one last Australian treat for Mandy and her dad. In a month's time, the Hopes would pack up and go back to England.

Mandy sighed. Home to Animal Ark, to Gran

and Grandad Hope and all her friends in Welford, the small village in Yorkshire where the Hopes lived. They would have to leave this vast, wonderful, colourful country behind.

Adam Hope kept the argument going. He wanted to make sure that Katie didn't doze at the wheel. 'And where else in the world would you find squirrels that fly?'

'New Guinea,' Mandy chipped in quietly.

'Hmph. And mammals that lay eggs?'

She knew that he meant the platypus; another Australian curiosity, with its duck-shaped bill and otter's tail.

'*And* 2000 kilometres of coral reef with millions of tropical fish? *And* the biggest rock on earth?' Gary added proudly. He told them about Ayers Rock, in the dead centre of Australia. 'It's about eight kilometres if you walk right round it, and it's 350-odd metres high; one single rock slap in the middle of the desert!'

'Sacred place for the Aborigines,' Katie said softly; 'I'll take you there next time you come.' She pulled at the wheel to avoid a spiny echidna which trundled across the road in front of them. They swerved back on to the road, just missing a battered metal sign. 'If you have a couple of weeks to spare, that is.'

Mandy read the notice: 'Watch Out For Kangaroos.' She leaned forward. 'Can you slow down a bit, Katie?' She was suddenly on the alert as she scanned the hillside for any sign of the roos.

'If I slow down any more, we might as well get out and walk the rest of the way!' Katie laughed. She tucked into the side, as another car came towards them on the single-track road. It roared by in a cloud of dust.

'How much further?' Mandy asked.

'Not far. About twenty kilometres to Mitchell, and then just five or six to the Gap.' Katie ran the back of her hand across her forehead, then grasped the steering-wheel once more.

'Want me to take over?' Adam Hope asked. They'd shared the driving on the long trip back from Melbourne.

She nodded and pulled off the road on to a rocky verge. 'Please. I'm whacked!'

They changed places, while Mandy and Gary peered into the valley ahead. 'Look, I can see the ocean!' Gary pointed to the right. Way in the distance there was a hazy blue line.

'I bet you can't wait to get there!' Mandy grinned at him. She knew Gary was surf-mad. He was in training for the junior boogie boarding championship next summer. It was impossible to keep him away from the beach and the high, rolling waves. Yet for four days he'd given up the surf and his board to come to the zoo.

'I could never drag him away for that long!' his mum, Abbie Simpson, had said, laughing.

His dad, Don, had winked and said nothing.

Since Mandy had arrived in Eurabbie Bay, Gary had discovered a new interest in animals, Don Simpson often teased. Now they didn't know if he would follow his dad's footsteps into the family swimming-pool business or if he would go to college and study to be a vet.

Mandy and Gary were best friends. He had shown her how to enjoy the outdoor life in Australia. She was a good boogie-boarder, thanks to Gary's coaching. It was one of the things she would miss when she went home to Welford.

Soon, with her dad in the driving seat for the final run into Eurabbie Bay, they were on their way again. Gary spotted the small town of

Mitchell, nestled between two tree-covered hills, and beyond that, way down on the distant coast, the bigger town of Eurabbie itself. 'Hey, my uncle lives up here some place,' he told them.

'I never knew you had an uncle!' Mandy was surprised. He never showed up at any of the Simpsons' barbecues by the side of their pool at Waratarah, their posh house overlooking Eurabbie Bay.

'No. It's my dad's brother, Uncle Art. We don't talk about him!' Gary went red and laughed it off. 'Forget I mentioned him!' He pushed his wavy sun-bleached hair back from his tanned face.

The car swayed and lurched over the rough road. 'Why?' Mandy hadn't pictured the Simpsons with a dark secret. Don and Abbie Simpson seemed ultra-respectable.

'We just don't have much to do with him.' Gary shrugged. 'They had a row about money when my grandpa died. He's got some farm or other up here. A couple of sheep, a goat, you know . . .' He trailed off again.

Mandy sighed. 'Here's me thinking you had a bank robber for an uncle, or something exciting like that!'

'Sorry, no. It's just boring old Uncle Art, with his beehives and his honey!' Gary hung on to the roll-bar as the Landcruiser tilted and dipped down a deep hole in the road.

'So why don't they make up the quarrel, then he could come over to Waratarah to visit?'

'I dunno. He reckons he doesn't have time.' Gary shuffled in his seat and stared out at the gum trees which lined the road ahead.

Mandy frowned. 'How can a couple of sheep, a goat and a beehive take up *all* his time?'

'Mandy!' Adam Hope gave her a warning glance. He changed the subject. 'Do I spy a buster gathering out at sea?'

They all craned their necks to see a tiny cloud forming on the horizon. The weekly storms would begin almost without warning; a puff or two of cloud, a couple of gusts of wind, then sudden downpour.

'Nah!' Katie crossed her fingers. A buster would force them off the road for an hour or two. 'Please don't rain on us now!'

Another cloud swept into view. 'No, not now we're nearly home!' Mandy cried. She longed to get home to her mum, a cold shower, and all the latest news about the patients in their kennels at the back of the surgery.

'Yep!' Gary confirmed with a nod. 'That's a buster all right!'

It took their minds off his Uncle Art. Adam Hope put his foot on the accelerator and tried to make it home before the storm.

'Kangaroos, Dad; remember!' Mandy warned. She saw one or two hop steadily across the road ahead. When she looked harder, she saw there were lots of them around, in the bush and loping by the roadside.

'Evening's their time for heading to the high ridges,' Katie explained. 'Mobs of sixty or more roos will go up into the hills for the night. They follow a set path, regular as clockwork.' She told them that this was when the 'Watch Out For Kangaroos' warnings were especially important.

Mandy felt herself tense up again. Another car had zoomed past in the opposite direction, trying to beat the storm. And now someone came lurching up behind, almost bumper to bumper with their own car. He hooted his horn to make them get a move on. She turned and glared.

Gary leaned out of the window and looked up at the sky. The two small clouds had quickly

gathered into a dark, angry mass that whipped across and hid the setting sun. Soon, the hills were in deep shadow. Big splashes of rain began to hit the windscreen. 'Here it comes!' he warned.

'Hang on, I'll just pull off the road here and let this chap through!' Mr Hope signalled and braked. But the road was too narrow, and it was too late for the impatient driver to beat the storm. The heavy, single splashes became a downpour. Rain battered on to the bonnets of the cars and turned their windscreens into waterfalls.

Soon, both Adam Hope and the other driver had to give in. They pulled into the side of the road together and sat under the gum trees, watching the road turn into a muddy, brown river.

'No one's going anywhere while this storm lasts,' Mr Hope said.

Mandy would have to wait a while for her home comforts. She stared out of the window at the blurred shapes of the poor wallabies. Further off, a herd of bigger kangaroos grazed miserably. There was nothing for it; they would have to wait for the buster to blow itself out.

Two

'Awesome!' Gary sat beside Mandy in the Landcruiser. Rain thundered down. It bounced off the car and on to the road. A wind roared and ripped leaves off the eurabbie trees. They spiralled into the rushing flood that had just now been the road.

'Pity you didn't bring your surfboard!' Mandy grinned. He looked as if he was enjoying the storm.

'Nice weather for platypuses!' In spite of the poor wet kangaroos, she felt herself relax. At least the rain would cool things down and give the herds of wallaby and kangaroo a chance to get clear of the road. Through the back window she glanced at the blurred, bad-tempered face of the driver in a hurry. 'But not nice weather for road-hogs!'

They sat for almost an hour, playing noughts and crosses on grids which they traced on the steamed-up windows.

Katie told Adam Hope more about her friend, Martin, whom they'd met at Melbourne Zoo. 'He took a vet's job there last year, after he did a special wildlife course at college in Sydney. He did a study on types of milk which they use to hand-rear orphan kangaroos,' she said.

'Yeah, why are there so many orphans?' Gary had noticed loads of joeys without mothers in the big nursery compound at the zoo. He knew they had to be reared on a bottle. 'Did their mothers get sick?'

'No. Traffic accidents mostly,' Katie explained. 'That's what kills off most mother kangaroos. The babies have to go to the zoo.'

'Don't!' Mandy shivered. Her own parents had been killed in a car accident when she was a tiny baby. Emily and Adam Hope had adopted her and given her a happy family to grow up in. She pitied the poor zoo orphans.

Katie went on. 'So, anyway, for this college study, Martin researched the protein a joey needs in its food. He came up with the perfect formula for artificial milk for one rare type of wallaby. It helped him get the job at the zoo.'

'It sounds like good work,' Adam Hope said. He glanced out of the window. 'Is it me, or is the rain easing off?' Water still slid down the windscreen, but it didn't batter so hard on the roof. The sky seemed to be clearing.

'Give it five more minutes,' Katie suggested. 'Then we can be on our way.'

'Not so much driving as white-water rafting?' Mr Hope got ready to start up the sturdy, four-wheel drive car. Behind them, the angry man roared his engine and flashed his headlights.

'OK, OK, no worries!' Katie wound down her window and yelled at him. 'Give us a chance, mate! The road's still a right mess!' She eased herself into her seat and shook raindrops from her short fair hair. 'Some people!'

Adam Hope grinned and signalled for the man to go first. They watched him ease his car on to the road, passing so close that the two wing-mirrors scraped.

'Idiot!' Katie muttered under her breath.

Mandy caught sight of a youngish man with long dark hair, wearing a green sweatshirt. His car was another off-roader; big and powerful, protected by the roo-bars that people fitted to their cars in case some careless kangaroo ran into their path.

'I hate those things!' Mandy said, watching the big silver car churn through the mud.

'What, the off-roaders?' Gary leaned over to see what she was looking at.

'No, the roo-bars.' Personally, she didn't think it was the kangaroos who were careless, so much as the humans who drove the cars.

'Why? A roo can make a pretty big dent in your car if you don't fit a roo-bar!'

'What about the dent a roo-bar makes in the poor kangaroo?' she said angrily. She watched the impatient driver pick up speed.

Gary shrugged. 'OK, but most people don't see it that way. Over here, you're not even supposed to swerve if a roo gets in your way. You're supposed to keep on driving, in case braking causes an accident.'

Up front, Adam Hope clicked on the Landcruiser's headlights. 'Dusk already,' he said quietly. Mist rose from the damp, warm earth.

The other car, red tail-lights winking, was already well down the road.

'He sure is in a hurry!' Katie frowned. They saw him lurch to the wrong side of the road, heard a squeal of brakes as he took a bend much too fast.

'I reckon the storm made him late for something pretty important.' Gary watched the red lights disappear from sight.

'He's going to crash if he doesn't watch out!' Mandy said darkly.

They drove on in silence. In the gathering dusk, they could see his headlights reappear and swing across the valley, then rise again up the next hillside.

'Watch out, Dad!' Mandy said suddenly. She saw five or six kangaroos taking mighty leaps across some open scrubland. They headed straight for the road.

'It's OK; I saw them.' Mr Hope checked in his mirror and braked. He came to a halt close to where the roos crossed the road ahead of them.

Mandy noticed that two of the mothers had tiny joeys peeping from the pouch, and one other was keeping a careful eye on a joey who was old enough to be out of the pouch, but not yet fully grown.

'What's she seen?' Mandy whispered. The mother roo had shuffled her joey towards the middle of the group as they all stopped by the roadside to graze.

'Dingoes,' Katie guessed. 'In those trees, I reckon.' She pointed to a group of shadowy eurabbie-gums.

And sure enough, a thin, lonely shadow prowled between the tall trunks. The dingo was a wild dog, skinny and yellow, with a long, bushy tail.

As the dingo left the trees, prowling nearer, the mother roo made a low chucking sound. The group quickly shied away from the trees, cutting across the clearing, up the hill towards the bare ridge.

Mandy's dad waited until they were safely out of sight and the disappointed dingo headed off elsewhere. Then he moved the Landcruiser on. Another car headed towards them, its lights glaring.

'We lost that other joker, at any rate,' Katie said. She meant the angry man who had spent the storm fuming behind them in his car. The muddy road bore the prints of his tyres, but no sign of the dipping, swaying lights.

But she spoke too soon. They climbed out of a valley, up the final stretch towards Mitchell, when they came across the silver car one last time. He seemed to have spun out of control and was pulling out of a ditch, reversing on to the road. His wheels whirred and threw up mud. The engine whined, the wheels skidded.

'Watch it, Dad!' Mandy cried, spotting him first.

'What the . . . !' Adam Hope braked.

Katie opened the door, ready to jump out and lend a hand, while Mandy and Gary sat tight, praying that no one had been hurt.

But just then the driver got himself straight and reversed back on the road. He changed gear and shot ahead, without waiting to speak to his would-be helpers.

'I reckon he took the bend too fast again,' Katie said, slamming the door.

Something; a feeling for trouble close at hand perhaps, made Mandy shake her head. 'No, I think it's more than that!' She leaned out, peering into the dusk. 'Dad, can you stop a minute?'

'What for?'

Her heart began to race. She saw a gang of kangaroos; maybe the same one as before, two with babies in their pouches, standing alert at the top of a rocky slope. Their dark silhouettes caught her eye. They seemed to be staring at the bend where the other car had come off the road. 'I think something bad has happened!' she whispered.

Without arguing, Adam Hope set his hazard lights flashing. All four of them climbed down on to the road. 'What do you reckon?' he asked Katie.

The nurse nodded. 'Mandy's right. Something spooked them.'

A couple of the roos shifted and called in distress. None moved from the flat rock as they gazed down on to the road.

'Over here!' Gary jumped into the ditch where the tyres had skidded out of control. 'Come quick!' He sounded shaken.

Mandy ran to the spot. She was right; there *was* something terribly wrong.

'That maniac, he hit a roo!' Gary gasped. His face was white, staring up from the dark ditch.

And now Mandy heard a soft whining sound

and she made out a shape in the ditch. A female kangaroo lay on her side, one foreleg covered in dark wet blood, and more blood coming out of her mouth in a slow trickle. 'Dad! Katie!' Mandy called.

'Don't move her, Gary!' she whispered, as he bent to try and straighten the poor creature. She pulled him back as the other two reached the spot and jumped into the ditch.

'What do you think?' Katie murmured as she clicked into action. She moved to one side to let Adam Hope check for a pulse.

'Pretty bad. She's not even struggling to get away.' Quickly he examined the injuries. 'Broken bones, severe shock and possibly internal bleeding.'

Mandy knew that an injured wild animal would try to run away if it could. Still, she prayed that her dad and Katie would be able to save the kangaroo. 'What should we do?'

Mr Hope made a split-second decision. 'Let's get her out of here. We need light and clean water. The car phone's out of action, and we need to phone the surgery to warn your mum!'

She realised that this meant the kangaroo would need an emergency operation. Emily

Hope would get everything ready to go ahead the moment they arrived at Mitchell Gap if only they could phone her.

'We'll lift her into the back of the car.' Mandy's dad waited for Katie to bring a blanket for use as a stretcher. Soon she came back and got into position. 'Where's the nearest farm, does anyone know?'

Gary and Mandy held the door open as the vet and the nurse gently rolled their patient on to the blanket and lifted it into the car. 'Yep!' Gary nodded, his voice low and anxious. 'That's Munroah, my Uncle Art's place, I reckon.' He pointed down the road.

'Good, you can show us the way!' Mr Hope ran to the front and jumped in. 'Climb up! Everyone ready?'

Mandy pulled the back door shut. She crouched with Katie beside the injured roo as Gary clambered forward to give her dad the directions he needed. 'That driver never even stopped to see if she was still alive!' she whispered, feeling tears sting her eyelids.

Katie muttered something, feeling for the roo's pulse, looking deadly serious. 'I knew he was an idiot!'

As they moved off, the kangaroo made a feeble attempt to lift her head. She struggled and gave up.

'What is it? What do you want?' Mandy turned and took a last look out of the back window at the scene of the accident; the skidding tyre marks, the smashed bushes. Up on the rock, the shadowy roos called out . . . 'Wait!' she cried.

Adam Hope braked again. 'Why, what's wrong?'

'Oh, look!' She pointed back down the road. A young kangaroo about the size of a small dog had crept out of the ditch. He stared at their disappearing car, caught in the gleam of moonlight that came out from behind a cloud.

The injured roo lifted her head, too weak to call out.

'It's her joey! She's a mother, and that's her baby!' Mandy grabbed Katie's arm. 'What'll we do?'

'Go get him!' Katie said without hesitating. 'He's not safe out there all by himself. A dingo could be on to him any minute!'

Mandy flung open the door and jumped out. She didn't stop to think, and the little joey seemed too shocked to move. She ran up to him, holding out both arms.

And the poor creature stood there stunned, letting himself be lifted off the muddy road and into the car. He clung miserably to Mandy as she carried him. She laid him down close to his mother.

'He's going to be all right, isn't he?' Mandy asked Katie. The Landcruiser eased forward at last. Gary sat up front and gave directions.

Katie looked down at her patient and breathed out slowly. 'I can't say for sure.' She stroked the little joey's head and turned to

Mandy. 'Good job you spotted him, though. I reckon there was a dingo out there waiting for you, little sunshine!' She stroked him again.

The joey's little black hands clutched hard at his mother's grey fur.

'No, not sunshine!' Mandy whispered. 'Moonbeam. I saw him in the moonlight. It must have caught his outline; that's how I spotted him, so that's what he should be called. Moonbeam.'

Katie smiled at Mandy. 'You saved his life; I reckon you can call him whatever you want! Moonbeam it is.'

Three

'This is it! This is my Uncle Art's place!' Gary leaned out of the car and pointed up the hill. In the back, Mandy sat stroking the joey, trying to keep him calm, as Katie did her best to keep the injured mother still and comfortable.

Art Simpson's farm was at the end of a rough track off the road just before they came to the town of Mitchell. 'Munroah'; the peeling sign swung from a tall mountain ash. It creaked in the wind.

Through the mud-spattered car window, Mandy caught sight of a battered old caravan resting on piles of bricks, two home-made wooden shacks made from other people's cast-off timber, and a row of white beehives. Tall, pale grass grew everywhere, and as she stepped down into a small clearing, she smelled the scent of a white bell-shaped flower that wound over the sheds and across the roof of Art Simpson's caravan home.

'You take the joey!' Katie told Mandy, and she handed out the trembling baby roo, as she and Adam Hope put their heads together to decide on their next move.

'I managed to stop the bleeding on the foreleg,' Katie told him. She'd applied a pressure bandage round the roo's arm.

'Yes, but it's the internal injuries we have to worry about.' He shook his head. 'Look, there's blood on her nose. That means she's probably bleeding inside her chest.'

Mandy cuddled the joey and walked further off. By the sound of her dad's voice she knew things were very serious. She followed Gary towards the door of his uncle's caravan. 'Is he in?'

Gary nodded. 'I can hear him now. Come on, Uncle Art!' he urged.

At last the wobbly door creaked open on its

hinges, and Art Simpson peered out into the darkness.

He looked nothing like his successful brother, Don, Mandy decided. He wore faded dungarees and a black T-shirt. His brown hair came to his shoulders. She expected him to have a shaggy beard, like an old ex-hippy, but he was clean-shaven, and his face was handsome. He had Gary's pale grey eyes and friendly smile.

'G'day!' he said, as if visitors dropped in at this remote spot every day of the week. 'Hey, Gary!' He slapped his nephew's shoulder. Then he spotted Mandy and the baby roo. 'You OK? Has your car been in a smash?' Quickly he took in the situation and came down the two rickety steps to ground level. 'Is that your Landcruiser?' he asked.

She nodded. 'There *has* been an accident, yes. But it wasn't our car. It was someone else; he was going too fast and he ran into a mother kangaroo. The road was bad after the buster.'

They led him across the yard. Mandy noticed a heavy shunting noise from inside one of the shacks, and in the moonlight she saw two thin black cats come slinking out of the long grass. From the shack, she heard the narrow, high snickering of a large animal. Moonbeam clung to Mandy's T-shirt and stared with his huge, startled eyes.

'That's Dollar,' Art explained. He strode ahead. 'My goat. I call him Dollar 'cos that's what he cost me. One dollar! His last owner wanted rid of him, see! Too noisy for the neighbours, he reckoned.'

Gary ran to keep up. 'We need to use your phone, Uncle Art! We've got the hurt roo in the car!'

Art nodded as Gary split off and ran back to the van. 'Is she really crook, the mother?' he asked Mandy. 'Is she bad?' He frowned as he strode on.

Mandy had no time to reply. As they drew near the Landcruiser, Katie and her dad straightened up at the same time. They'd been leaning into the car, tending the mother roo. Now they stood, hands on hips as if their backs ached, stretching and turning away. She stopped dead in her tracks. The joey wailed, as if picking up Mandy's own dread.

Adam Hope turned and spotted Art and Mandy. 'Too late,' he said quietly. 'There was nothing we could do.'

Katie turned away, looking up at the moon and stars.

Mandy let go of the one thin thread of hope she'd been clinging to; if they could only get the mother roo down to the surgery in time . . . if they could put her into Emily Hope's safe, calm hands, there on the operating table! But now, out here on the hillside, with the wind blowing and the darkness all around, all hope was gone.

Art leaned into the Landcruiser and nodded. 'Lift her out; I'll look after things if you leave her here.' His voice sounded quiet and sad. He hadn't asked who they were, or why they'd landed on him out of the blue.

Mr Hope nodded. 'Thanks. I'm Adam Hope, the vet from Mitchell Gap.'

They shook hands.

'Katie Browne. I'm the nurse there.' Katie nodded at Art. 'Gary brought us here. Sorry we bothered you.' She took a deep breath and began to pack away the first-aid bag.

'No worries,' Art told them. 'I'm sorry we couldn't do anything for the roo.' He frowned, then went on. 'I'll tell you something; I won't have a car on the place,' he said through gritted teeth. 'And this is why. I've seen too many roos killed on the road. And wombats, and wallabies; you name it!'

'No car?' Adam Hope looked round the untidy yard. 'You live here all alone?'

Art led him and Mandy back to his van, while Katie finished her work. Mandy still held Moonbeam close to her chest. He was heavy; over ten kilograms, she guessed, and her arms began to ache as he fidgeted and trembled with shock. He kept struggling to turn and look at the Landcruiser, where his mother lay, but Mandy held him fast and followed the two men.

'You might call it living alone,' Art went on. 'But I've got Ed and Al to keep me company, and—'

'Who?'

'The cats. And Dollar in the shack over there, and a few cows and sheep. I don't call that alone.' He led them up the steps into the van.

Gary looked round. He sat, phone in hand, waiting for the call to go through to Mitchell Gap.

'Never mind, Gary. It's too late,' Adam Hope told him quietly.

He put down the phone and hung his head.

'What about the joey?' He twisted his head sideways and looked up from under a creased brow.

Mandy held tight to Moonbeam. His dark, almond-shaped eyes stared into hers. 'We'll have to take him back to the herd, won't we? Someone there will look after him; another mother roo!'

Gently her dad shook his head. 'It doesn't work like that with kangaroos. This joey's on his own from now on.'

'But why?' She wanted a simple solution; take Moonbeam safely back to his mob, let him go, let the other roos look after him until he was big enough to take care of himself.

'Well, the other mothers have a lot on their hands rearing their own young,' Mr Hope explained. 'An orphan would just be allowed to starve to death.'

'You reckon he was still in the pouch?' Art asked. This would mean that the joey still needed his mother's milk. He cleared a space on a pile of floor-cushions for Mandy to sit with Moonbeam. His caravan was cluttered with books, fishing-rods, small wooden models of birds that looked hand carved.

Adam Hope nodded. 'He's just ten or eleven

months old by the look of him. Nearly ready to go it alone, but not quite.'

'How long will he last by himself on the food he can graze for himself?' Art stood, arms folded, gazing down at Moonbeam.

'A couple of days.'

'And what do you plan to do with him now?'

Mandy's dad glanced at his watch. 'It's pretty late. I guess we'll take him to our place for the night.' He turned as Katie came up the steps to join them. 'OK?'

She nodded. 'We can get going as soon as you like.' She smiled kindly at Mandy. 'I heard what your dad just said. No worries; we've got substitute kangaroo milk at the surgery. We can mix it and give it to him as soon as we get there. He won't starve, that's for sure.'

Mandy nodded. As she sat and stroked Moonbeam's soft fur, she still wondered if there was anything else they could have done. His wet nose nuzzled against her neck, his wiry arms clung tight.

'We'll have to check him out to make sure he hasn't got any cuts and bruises from the crash, then we'll probably get on the phone to Graham Masters at Peppermint Hill.' Mr Hope began to think ahead. He turned to Art Simpson. 'Graham runs the animal rescue centre. He's set up a compound to look after roos like this one. And kennels and so on.'

Gary's uncle listened carefully. 'You say you'll have to bottle-rear this little chap, is that right?'

'For a few days; until we're sure he can graze and feed himself properly.'

'Then what?'

Mandy heard Art asking the questions that buzzed inside her own head. This was the crunch; if Graham did look after Moonbeam at Peppermint Hill until he was properly weaned, what would happen to him after that? She knew Graham couldn't keep his fostered animals for ever. The rescue centre would burst at the seams if he did.

Adam Hope scratched his head and frowned. 'Then we put him back with the mob?' He turned to Katie, unsure of the answer.

'Maybe.' She shook her head. 'Maybe not. He might not be able to handle himself unless he has a mother to show him how. Have you ever seen joeys of his age? They're pretty wobbly on their legs, see. Little Moonbeam would be out of the pouch for short spells, learning the ropes;

how to run and kick, how to lie down, which is a pretty tricky thing with those enormous back legs of his getting in the way!'

Mandy felt Moonbeam settle in her arms. He clucked and sobbed, but grew calmer as Katie talked.

'Then Mum has to teach him the territory; how to stop, sniff, listen for danger. She shows him all the landmarks; the felled trees, the rocks he should recognise.'

It sounded complicated. Mandy glanced at Gary. Could an orphan roo ever hope to learn everything he needed to survive?

'And that's not all!' Katie spelt it out. 'Moonbeam's a male joey. He has to learn how to kick-box!'

'Kick-box?' Mandy echoed. Then she remembered; she'd seen the big males arch their backs and strut on their toes. They did it to show who was boss. If one male didn't give way, they fought it out by leaping and kicking with their back legs. Sometimes they would push and flick with their short forelegs, then lash out with their powerful back ones.

'Yep. It takes a lot of practice. His mum has to teach him.' Katie sighed. 'No, I reckon that what'll happen in a case like this is, they'll take the orphan joey to the zoo. It's probably the best thing.'

Adam Hope nodded. 'In Sydney?'

'That's the nearest,' Katie agreed. 'But Melbourne is the biggest. And I know Martin there would be glad to take the joey. Listen, I'll call him tomorrow and see what he says. Before you know it, we'll have young Moonbeam safe and sound in the nursery roo park in Melbourne. How does that sound?'

Mandy held her breath. 'You're sure he can't go free?'

She shook her head. 'It's a big risk, now that his mum's not around to keep an eye on him, believe me!'

'And we won't be here to see how things go, remember.' Her dad reminded her that their time in Australia was nearly up.

But Art Simpson didn't seem happy with the zoo idea either. '*I* will, though,' he suggested. 'I'm here day in, day out, looking after the sheep. In fact, I never leave the place. I go up the hill most days, or down by the creek fishing. Why can't I keep an eye on the joey?'

Mandy's hopes rose. Though Gary's family

had some old feud going with the smallholder, she decided she liked Gary's Uncle Art. She liked his ramshackle farm and cluttered caravan. Most of all, she liked the fact that he didn't drive a killer-car.

Katie frowned. 'You need a special licence,' she told him. 'If you want to hand-rear any marsupial in Australia, you need a permit from the government.'

Art chewed his bottom lip. 'That means filling out a form; that sort of thing?' He shrugged. 'I reckon I'm not one for filling out forms.' He let them know that he didn't like to get tangled up in anything official.

'That's a pity.' Mandy's dad rubbed his forehead. He looked tired. 'Keeping him here might have been the best idea.'

But Art Simpson backed off. 'Sorry,' he shrugged, scuffing the rug with the toe of his boot.

And so they stood up and shook hands. Art shyly asked Gary how his parents were getting along, but he made no mention of the family row.

Meanwhile, Mandy was forced to resign herself to taking Moonbeam to Graham's place at Peppermint Hill. He would be well-fed and looked after. From there, the joey would be driven away from his own grazing lands, far south down the coast, to the grand city of Melbourne and the zoo.

'The driver never even stopped!' Mandy told her mum. It was the one thing she couldn't forgive.

They bedded Moonbeam in a kennel in their residential unit for the night. Mandy fluffed up a bed of straw into a cosy nest. They'd checked him over as soon as they arrived. Though he was suffering from shock, there were no cuts and bruises.

'If you ran into something by accident, wouldn't you stop to see if there was anything you could do?' Mandy asked.

She put Moonbeam gently into the kennel. Katie had mixed a brand of milk powder and gave it to Mandy now.

'*I* would, yes,' Emily Hope agreed. She leaned one arm along the top of the kennel. 'But then, I know something about animals. I'd probably think I could do something to help. But this driver must have panicked. That's what happens when you feel helpless.'

Her mum's calm voice helped. Mandy began

to feel less angry. 'It's like running away because you're scared?'

'Exactly. He probably feels dreadful, wherever he is now.'

Mandy nodded. She tipped the bottle and sprinkled milk on to her wrist through the rubber teat. It seemed not too hot, not too cold, so she went ahead and began to feed Moonbeam. 'Here you are, drink this!' Gently she nuzzled the teat against his lips, tipping the bottle so the milk dribbled out. The joey sniffed and blinked. He opened his mouth and was soon sucking happily.

Emily Hope smiled. 'Well done. How about you? What do you want to eat?'

'I'm not hungry, thanks,' Mandy murmured. It had been a long day, and in some ways a terrible one. Now it was ten o'clock. Gary had gone home to Waratarah with his dad and Katie, who lodged with the Simpsons. Feeding Moonbeam was Mandy's last job before she collapsed on her pillow for the night.

'I'll make you something anyway,' her mum insisted.

Emily Hope had greeted them at the end of their long journey, standing by the pool in a loose, white cotton dress. She'd heard Mandy's story; all about Moonbeam and how he came to be an orphan. She'd been firm and kind. 'Another waif for you to rescue!' she smiled. Katie told her that it was Mandy who'd spotted Moonbeam and saved his life.

'Now it's time for *you* to be looked after!' she promised, going off to the house to make Mandy's supper. 'Don't be long here!'

Mandy fed the whole bottle of milk to Moonbeam. He drank greedily, head back, eyes closed. When he finished, she stroked his head and settled him into his bed. Then she fastened the kennel door and said goodnight. He was already half asleep when she walked down the row of kennels, past their resident patients.

There was a Labrador with a case of heartworm and a poodle with slug-bait poisoning. They had both been treated and were resting, getting better slowly. At the door, Mandy paused and turned to take a last look at Moonbeam. 'Goodnight,' she said again. He lay in the straw, long back legs stretched stiffly to one side, forelegs pointing to the front, head up, his eyes tightly closed. She smiled and turned out the light.

That night, after a supper of soup and bread, she went to bed and dreamed of young joeys climbing from their mothers' pouches, trying out their springy back legs, leaping, tumbling and bounding down a sunny hillside. They chased butterflies, ran too far, and returned to safety when their mothers called.

Four

Graham Masters said he would come to collect Moonbeam straight away. It was Easter, but Graham always worked through holidays. Easter was the same as any other time as far as animals were concerned.

'We're pretty full at Peppermint Hill,' he told Mandy on the phone. 'The land's parched after the hot summer, and the grazing's none too good. But I reckon we have room for one more little joey.'

Mandy stood in the surgery, watching Moonbeam scratch his sides with his sharp front claws. He stretched and gave a deep, short cough. She thought that this morning he seemed perkier, more interested in his new surroundings.

'Is that him I can hear in the background there?' Graham laughed. 'He sounds happy enough!'

'He is now that I've given him another feed!' She held the empty bottle in her spare hand.

'Have you tried him with hay?'

'Not yet.' Moonbeam had spent the night in the kennel. Now she'd opened the door and let him out on to the fenced yard at the back. He hopped up and down the run, stopping to scratch and cough. Hop, stop; take a curious sniff here, lope on, stop, look out of the yard up the hill at the creek. She smiled as she watched him explore.

Graham promised to bring some hay over with him. He asked if Mandy would like to drive back over to Peppermint Hill, to make sure that the roo settled in OK. 'If I know you, Mandy Hope,' he laughed, 'wild horses wouldn't keep you away!'

She laughed back. 'Thanks, Graham, I'd love to come!' Graham was one of the nicest people in Eurabbie Bay; kind and gentle with all the animals that were brought into the rescue centre. And he had a knack of knowing what she was thinking.

'I'll be right there!' he promised.

Soon he arrived in his Landcruiser, with a big cage for the joey to ride in, and a friendly smile for everyone at Mitchell Gap. Mandy caught sight of him from the run at the back of the surgery.

'G'day!' he called to Katie, hard at work in the kennels grooming Mitzi, the poodle. Her owner was coming to pick her up later that morning.

She waved back.

'How are you?'

'Good, good!'

Mandy saw him stroll into the surgery for a chat with Adam and Emily Hope. He was a tall, sturdy man with short, wavy hair. He always dressed in jeans and a checked shirt. He spoke quietly and slowly, never raising his voice. Animals were his life; rescuing them, looking after them in the big compound and the kennels at Peppermint Hill, then arranging for them to be fostered or adopted. He dealt with cats, dogs, possums and kangaroos; whatever people brought in, and always in the same calm, quiet way.

Finally he noticed Mandy still working with Moonbeam out back. 'G'day!' he waved, cool beer in hand.

She nodded and smiled. 'I can't believe this; he always seems to be hungry!' she called. Moonbeam was scratching for grass and nibbling whatever he could find.

'Go get some fresh hay out of the back of my car!' Graham said.

Mandy went to fetch the hay, grinning as Moonbeam pricked up his long ears and came loping along the run to meet her. 'You're certainly looking more lively!' she told him, as she went in through the wire gate and spread the bundle of sweet-smelling dried grass on the ground. 'Let's see how you get on with this.'

Moonbeam nipped at it at first, sniffed and listened, then tucked in.

Mandy loved watching animals feed. Moonbeam let her come up close, and she saw how he went on all-fours to seize the food and chomp at it, stuffing it into his cheeks and chewing slowly. Once or twice he reared on to his hind legs for a moment, for a quick, anxious glance around. Then, when Katie let Mitzi out into the open yard, he shied away and bounced off to the far end of the run, only hopping back when the coast was clear.

'Mitzi won't harm you!' Mandy laughed. 'She's more scared of *you* than the other way round!' She knew that most dogs would steer clear of those strong, kicking back legs. 'It's dingoes you need to watch out for.' She sighed. These were things a mother would teach a joey. 'And you've got to stay away from eagles too. And if a magpie starts screeching, that's a warning!'

Though he didn't understand, Moonbeam did come hopping back at the sound of her voice. He nuzzled and nipped at her T-shirt.

'Hey!' Gently she pulled free. 'I bet you didn't listen to a word I said!'

In answer, Moonbeam sprang into the air and twirled. He kicked out in play. Then he loped off after more of the sweet hay.

Soon Graham came out to join Mandy in the sunny yard. 'Right, mate?' He stood, hands in pockets, watching the joey polish off the hay.

'Yes, good. Mum says he should be OK now,' she told him. 'He wasn't hurt in the accident, so we think he can't have been in the mother's pouch when it happened. He was probably travelling solo!'

Graham nodded. 'Yep, he's a pretty big fellow.'

'Will he miss his mum?' This was one of her main worries; how Moonbeam would cope without his mother.

'Yep, I should say he will. They go by smell; I reckon he'll be sniffing round looking for her until he gets settled somewhere. And it works the other way round as well. I've known mother roos call out for their joeys for two or three days after the young one's died.'

'But do they get over it?' she asked.

'They do if they want to survive,' he told her. 'Any animal that's fit and healthy will fight to live, no worries.' He got to work. 'You want to go and fetch him? He knows you best. I'll open the cage.'

Mandy did as she was told. Moonbeam kicked out again when she went to pick him up. 'Come on,' she told him firmly. 'This isn't a game. We have to take you up to Peppermint Hill. You're going to like it there!' She tempted him with more sweet hay, and soon he was snuggled in her arms.

Quickly she carried him to Graham's

Landcruiser and put him in the cage. The door rattled shut. Moonbeam came and tugged at the wire, but Graham pulled the bolt across, and the joey retreated into a corner. At last they were ready.

'Don't worry,' Mandy told Moonbeam softly. 'This won't be for long. You settle down for a nap, and we'll soon have you in a nice new home.'

As usual, her voice seemed to calm him. He lay awkwardly in the straw that lined the bottom of the cage.

'OK?' Graham checked from his driver's seat.

She nodded and sat down next to the cage. She saw her dad standing at the surgery door to wave them off. 'I'll come up to Peppermint Hill and pick Mandy up after lunch!' he called.

'Yep, catch you later!' Graham called back, already on his way out of the gate.

As they drove, Mandy looked out on the dry hillside that dipped to the coast. She saw the narrow band of white sand, the stretch of blue ocean, and the town of Eurabbie nestling along its edge.

'I reckon you'll miss all this?' Graham said, reading her thoughts.

She nodded and sighed. There was less than a month left. With the breeze blowing through her blonde hair, the sun on her face, rescuing and taking care of animals like Moonbeam, Mandy felt she was in heaven.

The rescue centre was full, as Graham said. He decided to put Moonbeam into the big compound with over twenty other kangaroos and wallabies. 'He'll like it out in the open,' he explained. 'There are other joeys about his age, see.'

Mandy nodded and unlocked the cage. Moonbeam was eager to get out. Once more, Mandy lifted him and carried him, resting his weight on her hip, as if she was carrying a toddler. They followed Graham into a big fenced area and gently Mandy lowered the joey to the ground.

Looking round the compound, she spotted four or five roos the same size as Moonbeam. Two came hopping to meet him; long, thick tails thumping the ground, forelegs dangling. Moonbeam sat unsure, hovering beside Mandy. But the joeys were only curious. They sniffed and coughed, while Moonbeam crouched low.

'Friend or foe?' Graham grinned. 'If a roo crouches down like that, it means, "You're the boss!" He's letting them know he doesn't want to fight.'

Mandy nodded. At their full height, the two new joeys were nearly a metre tall. 'Thank heavens!' She didn't fancy having to get in there and separate them, like a referee at a boxing-match.

'They want to be your mates, see!' Graham smiled as they looked on at Moonbeam, who coughed and grunted.

The joey glanced over his sloping shoulder at Mandy, his rescuer. 'What now?' he seemed to ask.

She nodded. 'It's OK. You can go and play!'

He thumped his tail and sprang sideways. The other two followed. Then all three took off, their pale grey backs crouching forwards as they bounced up the sunny slope.

'That's Mitch and the other one's Star,' Graham told her. He pointed to Moonbeam's two new playmates. 'We found Mitch caught in razor-wire on a farm at Mitchell. And Star just wandered here all by himself one day last week. I don't know where he came from.'

Mandy began to feel sure that Moonbeam would like it here at Peppermint Hill. Though he would pine for his mum and the wide open spaces of the windy ridge, at least he wouldn't be lonely. 'I'm glad he's made friends,' she sighed.

'They usually do,' he told her. 'They like to belong to a gang. See that one?' Graham pointed to a fully grown roo nearby. 'That's Charlotte. Her problem is, she's too friendly. She trusts everyone, and she's had a couple of close shaves on the road by Waratarah because of that.'

Mandy nodded. Charlotte came up close and nosed at their pockets. 'So it's safer to keep her here?'

'That's right. Last time, she got a broken leg. She can't keep up with the mob any more. See, she's got a limp.'

Mandy scratched Charlotte's head and watched her move off to graze. Sure enough, the roo couldn't take her full weight on one back leg.

'That's the thing, see.' Graham led the way out of the compound, past rows of kennels, towards his office. 'Roos never think you're gonna harm them. They don't understand that people in cars won't slow down for them. They're about the most peaceable animals around, and tame. That's their problem.'

Mandy listened and learned, keeping one eye on Moonbeam as he settled into his new surroundings.

She spent the morning at the rescue centre; feeding dogs, dusting flea-powder on to stray cats, answering the telephone.

'G'day, Peppermint Hill Rescue Centre!' She picked up the phone in the office. Graham had gone out for an hour to buy feed and supplies in Eurabbie.

'G'day. I've rung about the joey,' a slow voice drawled.

'Which one?' Mandy was puzzled. Where had she heard this voice before?

There was a pause. 'His mother got killed in a car smash. Up at Munroah, last night.'

'You mean Moonbeam?'

'That's the one. I want to know how the little fellow's getting along.'

Mandy placed the voice at last. 'Mr Simpson, is that you?'

'Yep, Art Simpson speaking. Is that Gary's friend?' He sounded as if the phone might bite him; there were long, suspicious pauses between sentences.

'Yes, it's me – Mandy.'

'What can you tell me about the joey?'

'He's fine now. We brought him up here a couple of hours ago. He's out in the compound; I can see him now.' Moonbeam, Mitch and Star were grazing quietly in a little huddle.

Art Simpson grunted. 'You sure you're giving him the right feed?' he insisted.

'Yep. And he's made friends.' She couldn't help smiling. It sounded as if he didn't trust them to do it right.

'Friends? How many?'

She thought this was an odd question, but then Art Simpson was an odd sort of person. 'Two joeys. They're all about the same age. They seem to be getting on fine.'

'They're not fighting?'

'No, don't worry; he's going to be OK!'

'Good, good!' A long pause. 'Good! Two mates! . . . Catch you later!' Click. The phone went dead.

The smile faded from Mandy's face. It was nice of Art Simpson to take the trouble to ring up about Moonbeam, she thought. She would mention it to Gary when she saw him later that day.

But as she gazed out from the cool office up the hill to where the roos gathered in the shade of an enormous gum tree, she couldn't help feeling that the compound was still second best. Yes, Moonbeam had new friends, and yes, they'd managed to save his life after the terrible accident. Here he would be safe and well looked after until Graham decided it was time for him to be moved on to the zoo.

She stopped in the midst of this train of thought as she saw Moonbeam break away from his new mob of injured and orphaned roos. He leaped along the length of the fence, gazing out, stopping to call into the emptiness. No friendly voice answered back. His mother was dead, and his own clan now roamed far away, grazing, wandering.

And he would have to stay behind a fence for the rest of his life; half-tame, half-wild, looking out at the hillsides which were his true home.

Five

For three baking hot days over Easter, Mandy and Gary split their time between the beach and Peppermint Hill. They fussed over Moonbeam like anxious parents, preparing the bottle feeds and feeding him whenever he seemed hungry.

'When can we ease off?' Gary asked Graham. It was the third day after the accident. Heat rose from the dry earth in quivering, shimmering blasts.

'Soon. Another couple of days and we can stop the bottles altogether.' Graham glanced at Mandy. 'Cheer up, he's doing great!'

'I know.' Anyone could see that Moonbeam

was getting stronger. Now he was cheeky and confident, always on the move with Mitch and Star, really part of the gang. But Mandy realised that as soon as he was strong enough to move on, this phase of his life would come to an end. Meanwhile, Graham would be looking for two good homes for his new pals, Mitch and Star.

They spent the rest of that morning helping Graham to repair damaged fences at the rescue centre. Then, once the chores were done, he drove them down to the beach, to the rolling surf and sea breezes.

At teatime, Gary's mum picked them up and took them home to his house, tired but satisfied with their day. They drew up in the Simpsons' yard, ready for a drink and a cool shower.

'Make the most of it,' Merv Pyke warned. He was the local storekeeper and resident grumbler of Eurabbie Bay. His lean, grey figure and his white delivery van were a familiar sight. Now he watched, as Mandy and Gary unloaded their boogie boards from Abbie Simpson's car. He was delivering the daily order of fresh bread and milk to Waratarah. 'Summer's nearly over!'

Gary shrugged and shook sand off his board on to the patio.

'Gary, you watch where you're dumping that sand!' his mum yelled. With her sunglasses perched on top of her head, she ran indoors to answer the phone.

He took no notice. 'Race you into the pool!' he called to Mandy. He did a neat backwards flip into the cold, clean water.

Mandy dived in after him. She swam underwater until she felt her lungs would burst, then she bobbed to the surface.

Abbie Simpson came out with orange juice. 'That was your Uncle Art,' she told Gary with a puzzled frown. 'He *never* phones us!'

'What did he want?' Gary hooked his arms over the edge of the pool, letting the rest of his body float.

'Something about a joey? I don't really know. Was it something to do with the time you stopped off at his place last week?'

Mandy grinned. 'Moonbeam!' She squinted up at Mrs Simpson. 'He wants to know how our rescued joey is!'

'But he *never* phones us!' Abbie Simpson said again, going off and shaking her head. 'Not since your grandpa died, and that was six years back.'

The phone rang again. This time it was

Mandy's mum. Mrs Simpson came back this time with a complicated message. 'Your mother says Graham rang to tell Katie that Martin from Melbourne is driving up to Eurabbie tonight. Does that make any sense?' She flopped on to a sunlounger and began to flick through a magazine.

Mandy thought it through. 'Yes. That must be Katie's friend, Martin, the one who works at the zoo.' Things slotted into place and her heart sank. These were facts that she'd rather not think about. 'You know, she told us about him; how he might be able to take Moonbeam back to Melbourne.' Things were moving faster than she expected. She hauled herself out of the water and reached for a towel.

Gary followed. 'I reckon it had to happen sooner or later.' He looked at her. 'You OK?'

Mandy shivered, in spite of the heat. Things changed, nothing went on for ever; she knew that. But she wished they could have had a few more days with Moonbeam. 'Just when he's made good friends with Mitch and Star!' she whispered. 'Now he'll have to go off to the zoo all by himself and start again!'

'Let's go and see?' Gary suggested.

She hesitated, then nodded. She would want to say goodbye to Moonbeam, and this might be their last chance.

Abbie Simpson glanced up from the fashion pages of her magazine. 'I'll drive you,' she offered kindly. 'We should get up to Peppermint Hill just after tea.'

So they drove up to the rescue centre, quiet and nervous, accepting that it had to happen.

If a joey has to be an orphan, I guess Peppermint Hill is the best place to take him, Mandy consoled herself. *And if he has to spend the rest of his life in a zoo, I guess Melbourne is the best there is.*

She tried to look on the bright side, but there was a lump in her throat as Mrs Simpson drove her sleek estate car through the wooden gates of Peppermint Hill.

Katie was there, and Graham, and a young, dark-haired man in a crisp white shirt and dark trousers. They stood by the entrance to the kangaroo compound, all with their arms folded, talking seriously. Graham turned and waved as he heard their car. He strode over to meet them.

'You got the message?' He held open Mandy's door as she climbed out. 'It all happened pretty quick. Martin rang to say his zoo has space for three new roos. Katie said he should come straight up and take a look here.' He led Mandy and Gary to meet the young vet. 'It's just as well; we really need to find homes for these young joeys!'

'Did you say the zoo has room for three?' Gary asked.

'That's right.' Graham seemed pleased. 'Melbourne can take all of them; Moonbeam, Mitch and Star. They can stay together!'

'Wicked!' Gary said. He nodded hard at Mandy.

'Yep!' she agreed. 'That's fantastic.

It makes sense, she told herself firmly. *At least Moonbeam won't be lonely.* Still, she was sad as she picked him out from the mob; his pointed face, his long ears and soft white chest. She saw him bound eagerly down the hill towards her, with Mitch and Star close behind.

'Mandy, this is Martin Reed.' Katie introduced them. 'And, Martin, this is Gary Simpson. Martin says these joeys would be ideal for the zoo,' she explained. 'They're feeding by themselves now. He wants to take them back with him tomorrow morning.'

Mandy nodded and tried to smile. *This is it!*

Things were going on round her in a kind of dream. She went to the fence and stroked Moonbeam's soft black nose, smiling as Mitch nudged him to one side. Moonbeam scuttled back into position, his big eyes fixed on her as she reached through the fence once more to stroke behind his ears.

'We'll take good care of them, no worries,' Martin said. 'You saw the roo compound at the zoo, didn't you? It's the most modern in the world. The roos live practically free, like on a safari park.' He came up to Mandy. 'I reckon you'll miss this chap, though?'

She nodded, but she didn't trust herself to speak. She went on stroking Moonbeam, feeling his rough tongue lick her hand.

'Come on inside and have a beer,' Graham suggested to Martin. 'And do you two want a Coke?' he said to Mandy and Gary. He waved Abbie Simpson to come into the office. Then he stopped in the doorway. 'Wait up a second!' He wrinkled his eyes and stared out of the gate, up the hill. 'Who's this?'

Katie and Martin had disappeared inside the office with Gary's mum, but Mandy and Gary waited with Graham on the verandah.

'Uh-oh!' Gary gasped, then whistled. 'I reckon that's my Uncle Art!'

A figure tramped steadily down the dusty road. He wore a wide-brimmed bush hat, faded dungarees and boots.

'It is!' As he drew near, Mandy recognised the shy smile and clear grey eyes of Gary's uncle. 'He's come to visit Moonbeam, I bet!' she gasped. She remembered his anxious phone call and his kindly interest in the orphan joey.

'G'day!' Art Simpson mumbled shyly. He stood and brushed the dust from his hat, trying to ignore their surprise. He took a good look round the rescue centre.

'Uncle Art,' Gary said, as shy as his retiring relative.

'Gary.'

Mandy realised that the two of them could stand there all day, grinning awkwardly. 'We never thought we'd see you over here. How did you get here?' she asked.

'Walked.'

'All the way from Munroah?' She guessed it must be ten or twelve kilometres.

'Yep.'

'In this heat?'

'Yep. I came to see the joey.'

'He's over here.' Mandy smiled and offered to lead the way. She noticed Abbie Simpson, cool and elegant in her blue summer dress, come out onto the verandah.

'Is that you, Art?' she said in a peculiar, high voice.

Gary split off to explain to his mum.

'You only just got here in time,' Mandy told their visitor. 'The vet's come up from Melbourne. He's taking Moonbeam to the zoo tomorrow.'

'The zoo?' Art Simpson's springy stride came to a halt. He stood, chewing gum, considering this latest development. 'You reckon?'

'He can't stay here.' Graham came up to help Mandy out. 'We have to foster some of these roos out to make space for new ones.'

'Foster?'

'Or get them adopted.' Graham nodded.

Mandy stood and listened quietly.

'Adopted?'

'Yep. But you need a licence to own a kangaroo. They're protected. It's so we can check the owners, see.' Graham was patient as he told Art the rules.

'Yep, a licence. I know all about that.' Art nodded. He turned to Mandy. 'You were right, I reckon I got here just in time.'

'How come?' She watched Art Simpson dig into the bib-pocket of his baggy dungarees. He pulled out a creased piece of paper and began to straighten it out.

'Like I said before, I'm not one for filling out forms,' he reminded her. 'But I thought about it long and hard, and I reckoned if that's what it takes . . . then that's what I gotta do!' He handed the crumpled paper to Graham.

Graham read it. 'This sure looks to me like a

licence to keep kangaroos!' he said slowly. He glanced up at Art. 'Is it all fair and above-board?'

He handed the licence to Mandy, who read it through. 'Gary!' She called across the yard, signalling wildly for him to come. She dashed to meet him, waving the paper at him. 'Your Uncle Art wants to adopt Moonbeam and take him back to Munroah!' She dragged him towards the two men, wondering who would have first claim; the zoo vet or the smallholder?

'I reckon my place is better than a zoo any day,' Art Simpson said. Mandy noticed that a stubborn streak had begun to show through his shyness as he argued it out.

'Yeh, but why *this* joey?' Graham pointed to Moonbeam.

'*Because*!' Art outstared him. 'My place is where he belongs! That's where his mob is, and that's where I want him to be.'

'OK.' Graham understood this. 'But you know it means taking him away from his mates?' He pointed to Mitch and Star, who crowded round Moonbeam by the fence.

'No, that's not right either,' Art protested. 'Look at the licence. It says I can look after three joeys. The Munroah joey and two others, see!'

He stood firm. 'The permit says I can look after three. I heard Moonbeam had a couple of mates.' He broke off to glance at Mandy, who smiled back and nodded. 'So that's what I got on the licence; *three* roos!'

Mandy studied the paper which she still held in her hands. She saw it plainly in black and white; a permit to look after three kangaroos. 'Moonbeam, Mitch and Star!' she gasped. 'Please, Graham! Mr Reed can take three other roos to Melbourne, can't he? Then you'll have even more room here at the centre!'

Slowly Graham looked round the group. 'Wait here.' He went into the office to discuss it with Katie and Martin Reed.

Meanwhile, Abbie Simpson came up to her brother-in-law. 'G'day, Art,' she said shyly.

'G'day, Abbie.' He greeted her with a short nod.

'How are things?'

'Good, good.'

'It's been ages . . .' She looked guiltily at Gary and Mandy, lost for words.

'Yep,' Art agreed.

'Look, about this silly argument between you and Don . . .'

'Say, I don't want to talk about it right now, Abbie.'

'No, listen, it's high time you two got together and made things up. After all, it was only money you argued about, wasn't it? And blood *is* thicker than water, you know. You two are brothers.'

'You reckon?' Art stared steadily at the ground.

'I know so. Look, why not come over to Waratarah for a meal?'

'Will do, if I get the time, mate.'

As he tried to worm his way out of Mrs Simpson's invitation, Mandy pictured Art sipping fancy cocktails by their pool. She smiled to herself, unable to imagine him in his dungarees chatting to Don and Abbie Simpson's smart friends.

At last, Graham emerged from the office with Katie and Martin. 'Here they come!' Gary whispered.

All heads turned to look.

'That's fine,' Graham was saying. He walked up to Art. 'Martin will take three of the other young roos. It turns out we can make everyone happy.'

'I can take the ones I want?' Art said slowly.

'I reckon so.'

Mandy heaved a sigh. 'Wicked!' she whispered at Gary with a glint in her eye. She looked on his Uncle Art as a kind of wizard, appearing out of nowhere, waving his licence like a magic wand. 'How will you look after them?' She wanted to know exactly what would happen to Moonbeam, Mitch and Star now.

'I already built a compound,' Art said, matter-of-fact. 'Out of some spare timber and wire. But I plan to get them back with the mob in the long run.' For him it was a long speech. 'Back where Moonbeam belongs.'

It sounded perfect. All her dreams for the orphan roo could come true after all. She wanted to fling her arms around Art and hug him. 'Can we visit? Can we help?'

'Sure. You fix things with your folks.'

'Mum?' Gary stepped in quick as a flash. 'I can help Uncle Art with the joeys, can't I?'

Mrs Simpson wore an expression that said that nothing could surprise her any more. 'It'll mean less time on the beach,' she reminded him.

'I know, but this is important, Mum.'

Mandy nodded and held her breath.

'I don't see why not,' his mum said slowly. Then she turned to her brother-in-law. 'You sure you don't mind having them come to visit?'

'Glad of the help,' he said. 'Any time.' He gave them one of his shy grins. Then he knitted his brows and coughed. 'As a matter of fact, I need a favour,' he told Abbie.

'Yes?' She seemed anxious to help.

'Can you give us all a lift back to Munroah, me and the joeys?' he said, slow and thoughtful. 'What do you reckon; can we stick them in the back of your car? It won't mess it up too bad, will it?'

Abbie Simpson smiled weakly. 'I reckon not.' She went to spread newspaper in the back of the gleaming car.

Mandy watched happily as the joeys played together, the grown-ups sorted themselves out, and Art fixed up luxury transport for his new little clan of kangaroos.

Six

'The trouble with Art is that he doesn't move with the times,' Abbie Simpson told Emily Hope. 'It can be a bit embarrassing, you know.'

Mandy watched her mum's face. The two women were driving Gary and Mandy to Munroah for the first time, loaded with things they would need to help Art look after the joeys at the smallholding. It had all happened as planned. Art's shy invitation to them to help settle the joeys into their new home was accepted, and all the arrangements to spend a day on his hillside farm were made.

'You know, sometimes I think that the times

we live in aren't worth moving with,' Emily Hope replied. She gazed peacefully along the groves of nut trees, across open fields of pale yellow wheat. 'I envy people like Art. His life's so simple. Somehow he seems to have worked things out better than most of us.'

Mrs Simpson's car drew to a halt under the creaking sign for Munroah. 'Even before the big family bust-up, I always thought he was a bit, well, eccentric,' she confessed. 'But I reckon it takes all sorts.'

'Here's Dollar!' Mandy saw the goat's head appear over his wall and bray.

'He's checking up on us!' Emily Hope smiled at the grizzled old goat.

Mandy clambered out of the car and ran to say hello. Dollar stamped his hooves and snickered, then raided her pockets for treats. 'Here you are!' She gave him a mint. Dollar nodded and swallowed it whole.

'That's OK, then.' Gary grinned. 'It looks like we can stay!' He stood getting his bearings in the overgrown yard.

'Better take these.' His mum came up gingerly, keeping her distance from the greedy animal. She handed Gary a whole bagful of sweets.

Dollar already had his eye on them. 'Where's Art got to?' The caravan looked deserted, except for the two black cats who sat on the top step, soaking up the sun.

'There he is!' Mandy pointed to one of the fields behind Dollar's. She'd spotted Art leading his tiny herd of sheep down the hill towards them. 'Hi!' she called. 'How's Moonbeam?'

'Good!' He came on down, unhurried, leading the sheep into Dollar's field.

Quickly Mandy and Gary unloaded the joeys' extra hay. They said goodbye to their mothers and arranged to be picked up again after dark. Then they dashed off to see where Art was keeping the joeys.

'Behind the orchard,' he told them. He pointed towards a narrow creek and a slope of apple trees, where the fruit ripened to a russet gold in the late summer sun.

They jumped the stream and ran between the trees. There, on the open hillside, fenced in by a modern electric fence, they found the three joeys happily grazing. Mandy spied their rounded backs, the long, thick tails, the lowered heads. 'Moonbeam!' she called softly.

His ears pricked and swivelled as he

recognised her voice. He came bounding towards them, while Mitch and Star followed more warily.

Mandy stretched an arm through the fence to stroke Moonbeam's ears. He bent his head and grunted quietly.

Then they fed the joeys with juicy grass that grew out of reach beyond their fence. Soon, Art came along to join them.

'This is great for the joeys!' Mandy told him. She laughed as Moonbeam jumped and gave Star a friendly kick on the rump. Then the two young kangaroos wrestled. Mitch strutted alongside.

'Who's the boss here?' Gary asked. He'd pulled a blade of grass and let it hang from one corner of his mouth, chewing the sweet end.

'Moonbeam,' came Art's prompt reply. 'He wins all the kick-boxing contests.'

Just then, as Star crouched and gave in, Mitch came and landed a hefty thump on Moonbeam's rear-end.

'Don't speak too soon!' Mandy laughed. The two joeys began to wrestle, arms locked, rolling on the dusty ground.

Art grunted. 'We wouldn't want him to get

too big for his boots.' He stood back and watched the play-fight, thrusting his hands deep into his pockets. 'I took the sheep out of this field and put the joeys here because it backs on to the roo track,' he explained.

'Isn't it too dry?' Mandy asked. No rain had fallen since the day of the accident, and the grass was bleached almost white in the heat.

'No, the roos get by on it, no matter how dry it gets,' Art told her. 'Like I said, he can see his mob from here. At dawn, they come down into the valley. Then at dusk, they use the same track to go back on to the ridge.'

He pointed out landmarks that the mob used to find their way; another creek, almost dry at this time of year, that trickled between yellow rocks, and a big outcrop of darker, reddish stone that stood out from the green bush. The rock was a major landmark for the roos as they came up from the valley. 'They follow that track, day in, day out,' Art said. 'I want these three joeys to get used to seeing them come and go.'

'So they can join the mob themselves eventually?' Mandy asked.

'Yep. When they're ready.'

'When will that be?'

'A week. Maybe two. We've gotta build them up first.'

Gary grinned. 'They look pretty fit to me.' The young roos were leaping and scrambling all over one another.

'Good feed,' Art said, coming straight to the point as usual. 'That's what they need.'

'We brought extra hay,' Mandy told him. 'Graham says it's exactly what joeys need at this age; plenty of good quality hay.'

Together they made plans for Moonbeam, Mitch and Star. Then they took a rest from the heat by going down to Art's caravan for cold drinks. Mandy and Gary sat in the shelter of a shady nut tree, close to the animal shacks; there was no room in Art's cluttered van for two extra people to sit and relax.

They spent the rest of the day taking hay feeds to the joeys and helping Art with chores round the farm. They discovered that, though his place looked a mess, there was method in everything; a time to collect honey from the hives, a time to move the sheep from one pasture to another.

Art followed his routine with a steady patience, finding a few minutes here and there to sit in the sun with Ed on his lap and Al curled at his feet. He would sit with his cats and whittle away at a block of wood that slowly took shape as a cockatoo. Every so often, Mandy would remember Dollar and slip off to his field to feed him a mint.

In the evening, Art took them to look at the roo track. They climbed the hill beyond the far creek and stood on the outcrop of dark rock, waiting for the mob to follow their evening trail.

Soon, they came out of the valley; roos of all sizes; four males and dozens of females with their babies. They grazed as they went, alert to Mandy, Gary and Art, but more interested in the three joeys behind the fence, who sat and watched them go by.

'Won't we scare them off?' Mandy asked, surprised that the roos had come so close.

'No, they don't mind us. Just watch this,' Art said under his breath.

One male roo, the boss of the whole herd, approached the fence and began to strut. Mitch backed off, but plucky Moonbeam reared up and arched his back.

'Good job he's behind that fence!' Gary laughed. Moonbeam was half the size of the wild male.

'Pick on someone your own size,' Mandy told him. She enjoyed the wind that had got up; it blew her hair from her face and cooled her skin. Cheeky Moonbeam leaped up the hill, showing off his speed to the older kangaroo. Then he loped back to face the boss male.

But the other male soon lost interest in Moonbeam's playful game. He had to see to the serious business of getting his mob up the hill before dark. And tonight there was a challenge from another junior roo; a strong young male who wanted to knock the leader off his perch.

'Now this looks a whole lot more serious,' Art said, his voice suddenly tense.

Mandy and Gary saw the mob grow edgy. Mothers rounded up their joeys and called the smallest ones to their pouches.

'I reckon the youngster fancies his chances,' Art warned.

From inside the compound, Moonbeam, Mitch and Star sniffed anxiously. They stood and watched the battle from a safe distance.

First, the challenger reared up to his full height, chest out, head back. The boss charged at him for his strutting cheek. He forced him to the outside edge of the mob. Females clucked and skittered out of the way. Then the young male turned and stood his ground. He pushed at the boss with his full weight, avoiding flicks from his opponent's sharp front claws. The boss male jumped at him with his back feet. He missed, giving the challenger the chance to lash out and grab the boss's head and neck.

'Ouch!' Gary watched the challenger swing the leader to the ground. Then the big male twisted free and was up on his feet in a flash, charging and kicking. At last, he landed a hefty thump.

'Those legs can do a lot of damage,' Art told them. 'I've seen them finish off a dingo in one go!'

Mandy held her breath. 'Who's going to win?'

'The boss, I reckon. See, the fur's starting to fly.' He kept his voice steady, though the action grew wild.

Mandy winced and blinked.

The boss lunged at the challenger and seized him by the neck. 'Look, he's going for a headlock,' Gary said.

'He plans to kick him when he's down.' Art kept his eye on the two contestants. 'See, the youngster isn't strong enough.'

Mandy forced herself to watch the furious contest. At last, after much kicking and swiping with the dangerous claws, the challenger had had enough. He crouched low to the ground and coughed.

'That's him kowtowing,' Art explained. 'It's the signal to show he knows who's boss.' He turned to Mandy. 'It's OK, they haven't drawn blood; not this time!' He summed up the look on her face. 'You're thinking that this is what Moonbeam's gonna be up against.'

She nodded. 'It's tough being part of a mob, isn't it?' She hadn't realised that these graceful, inquisitive creatures also had an aggressive side.

'You're right there,' Art agreed. He nodded at the three youngsters inside the compound. 'If the boss male felt like it, he could chase them out of the mob, no worries.'

'And does a roo definitely need a mob?' Gary asked.

'They wouldn't get far without one,' Art replied. 'They get their strength in numbers, like all herding animals. One by himself would soon be picked off by a dingo, for instance.'

Gary whistled low and soft, then glanced at Mandy. 'We'd better pile on the protein,' he told her. 'These joeys need a lot of building up before we let them loose!'

They promised to help Art every step of the way. 'Try stopping me!' Mandy told Gary's uncle. She smiled happily and went about the task of taking feed up to the joeys' compound.

What's more, she found that Art was on the same wavelength. He seemed to understand what Moonbeam had been through. 'Losing his mother set him back. He won't put on weight so fast, and he won't learn all the tricks he needs to survive at the same rate as a wild joey,' he told her.

It was true that Moonbeam seemed to need Mandy's company more than the other two joeys, perhaps because he still missed his mother. He came and sat with her, happy to groom and scratch while the others played.

And when she feared that a half-tame joey would never make it, that he was too cheeky or not brave enough to survive in the wild, Art would say, 'Give him chance. Rome wasn't built in a day.'

Nothing upset Art, or threw him out of routine. Quietly, steadily they built Moonbeam up. 'Soon,' he promised. 'We're getting there slow but sure.'

Mandy listened and learned.

She and Gary worked hard on the joeys for more than a week. Day by day they saw a difference; Moonbeam was definitely bigger, stronger, and his awkward, jerking leaps, all legs and feet, had become smooth bounds.

At midday on the seventh day, as they stood with Art quietly watching the joeys graze, a magpie suddenly flew noisily from a gum tree and Moonbeam and his mates broke off feeding.

'Watch this,' Art whispered.

Moonbeam's head was the first to go up. His ears twitched nervously. Mitch and Star huddled behind him as the bird cawed loudly overhead.

Mandy caught sight of a movement in the pale grass beyond the compound. A dingo crouched nearby, tongue lolling in the heat. Moonbeam spotted him. Quick as a flash, he led the joeys away down the hill.

'That's it, that's the idea,' Gary breathed.

The dingo crept off on another silent hunt.

'He recognised the danger.' Mandy was

pleased by how well the joeys had taken care of themselves.

'Tomorrow, then,' Art said with a firm nod.

'Tomorrow?' Mandy knew what he meant, but she wanted to hear him say it out loud.

'Tomorrow we set them free.'

Half-proud, half-sad, Mandy went home to tell her dad what they'd decided.

Mr Hope looked pleased. 'Great. Well done. It takes a lot of patience to look after three young roos. Listen, can I come up with you? I'd love to see how it goes.'

Mandy was thrilled. 'Yes!' She rushed on, telling him all their plans. 'We can't leave it any longer because of this dry weather we're having.' The land was more parched and scorched than ever.

'How come?' Adam Hope rocked in a chair on the quiet verandah. The sky was starlit, the moon was new.

'Art says the grass in the roo compound won't last much longer. He wants the joeys to go down to the river flats with the rest of the mob; there's better grazing down there.'

'Well, he's probably right. I heard a drought warning on the radio this afternoon,' he told her. 'They've brought in a hosepipe and sprinkler ban, and now they're worried about forest fires too. They say it could get bad.'

She nodded again. 'That's why we want to make it sooner rather than later. Art has hay in one of the shacks, but that's for Dollar. He can't spare any for the joeys.'

'How worried is he about this drought?'

'Well, you know him. Art never looks worried, but I reckon he is, deep down.' Mandy realised that Art had spent a lot of time lately gazing at the clear blue sky and checking the weather forecasts.

'The trouble is, the wind's in the wrong direction,' Mr Hope said. 'It's coming straight off the desert; no rain there, I'm afraid. And none for a good few days by the sound of things.'

'Well, anyway, tomorrow is Moonbeam's big day!' It was a Saturday, and she and Gary had agreed to meet up early. Mandy looked forward to it with mixed feelings, knowing that this could be her last chance to get close to Moonbeam.

'Well, I'll give you a lift.' Adam Hope looked long and hard at Mandy. 'How are you feeling about it?'

'Good.' She nodded. She didn't want to talk.

He grinned. 'You sound like Art Simpson!'

Mandy took this as a compliment. 'Do I?'

'Yep. Not saying much, just getting on quietly, doing what has to be done.' He went and put an arm round her shoulder.

'Thanks, Dad.' She looked up at him.

'For what? Saying you sound like Art?'

'No.' She smiled. 'To you and Mum, for bringing me to Australia.' Tomorrow, at Munroah, when they let Moonbeam go free, would be the first of many goodbyes.

'Let's all go up,' Mr Hope suggested; 'you, your mum and me. The whole family.' He was halfway through the door when he had another idea. 'And maybe the Simpsons as well; Don and Abbie as well as Gary. We could take a picnic.'

Mandy shook her head. 'Gary's dad and his Uncle Art aren't speaking. There's no chance of Mr Simpson wanting to come up there on a picnic with us.'

'Why's that?'

Mandy heard her mum wander out on to the veranda.

'Apparently there was a fight over their father's will.' Emily Hope sat in the chair and began to rock. 'According to Abbie, Art and Don each got half of the old man's money. Art promptly announced that he didn't need his share and gave the whole lot away.'

Adam Hope whistled. 'Who to?'

'To a small wildlife charity up in Queensland. He said the charity needed the money to help preserve the jungle habitat more than he needed it to improve his smallholding. Don was furious.'

'Why?' To Mandy, Gary's Uncle Art had done exactly the right thing.

'Abbie says Don was in bad financial trouble himself right then. He could have used every dollar of the old man's money that Art chose to give away. It took him five years to get his business back on its feet.'

'And is he still mad?' Mr Hope asked.

'Don says Art is just a dreamer. But Abbie thinks that he misses him really, only he's too proud to admit it.'

'Like Gary's uncle,' Mandy sighed. 'He's proud too.' She thought of the two brothers and the family that had been split up for far too long.

Mr Hope came and ruffled a hand through her hair. 'There's no point worrying about it. There's nothing you can do.'

'No?' Suddenly she jumped up and ran inside.

'Mandy, what's going on?' her dad called. 'What are you up to this time?'

'Nothing!' she yelled back. 'I just have to make a couple of phone calls, that's all!'

Seven

'Pass the bread and honey, honey!' Adam Hope called. He sat, dangling his feet in the cool water of the creek at the back of Art's place. 'This home-made stuff is delicious!'

Mandy took him the slice of bread and sat down beside him. The bread oozed golden honey.

' "Isn't it funny . . ." ' he began.

'What?'

How a bear likes honey!
Buzz, buzz, buzz . . .
I wonder why he does!

* * *

Mandy laughed. 'Dad, how many pieces have you had?'

'Four.' He edged sideways along the bank to make room for her.

'This picnic was a good idea, wasn't it?' She settled down beside him.

'Pretty good,' he admitted with more than a touch of pride. It had been his idea in the first place.

'Pretty good! This was an utterly *amazing* idea,' said Mandy. 'Getting the Simpson family together for the first time in ages, sitting chatting in the sun, drinking home-made wine, blah, blah . . .'

'I thought you said that Don and Art would never agree to it,' he said, suddenly suspicious. 'This couldn't have anything to do with the phone calls you made last night, could it?'

Mandy glowed with pleasure. 'It could have!'

'Mandy?'

'Aren't you going to ask me how I did it?' she asked, her eyes twinkling.

'OK, Mandy, how did you do it?'

'Easy. First of all I rang Art and told him that Gary's dad was keen to come up and take a look at the joeys before we put them back with the mob.'

Mr Hope stared. 'And then?'

'Then I rang Mr Simpson and told him that Art had invited them all up to Munroah for a picnic.' She gave her father a sweet smile.

'And they believed you?'

'They couldn't wait. All they needed was the chance to get back together, but neither would make the first move. I just helped things along a bit, that's all.'

They turned to watch the two brothers deep in conversation. Mandy's white lie had worked perfectly.

'Mandy Hope, did you know something's happened to your nose today?' Adam Hope asked.

Her hand flew up to her face. 'No, what?'

'It's grown several inches longer, just like Pinocchio's!'

'Dad!' She splashed water at him with her feet.

He laughed and glanced over his shoulder. 'When are we going to take a look at those joeys?'

'When you're ready.' She judged from the height of the sun in the sky that it would soon set. Then the time would be right to set the joeys free.

'Well, look, why don't you and Gary go ahead now, while we oldies stay here and clear away our mess?' He stood up and helped her to her feet. 'Go on, we'll follow you.'

Mandy took a look at the group still sitting and chatting under the shade of the tall mountain ash tree. A cloth was spread on the grass, piled with bread, cheese and cake brought along by Abbie Simpson and Emily Hope. Art had added the extras; honey, fruit, wine and fruit juice.

The picnic was going well, she had to admit. Don, Abbie and Art were still busy catching up on one another's news. So far, the family get-together had gone without a hitch. Mandy slipped her feet into her canvas shoes. 'OK,' she said. She went to drag Gary away from the food. 'Let's go!' she gestured towards the hill.

Soon they were on their way; taking a last chance to get close to Moonbeam and his two pals. They slipped between the shacks, towards the fields.

'Art says we just have to hit the right moment when the mob treks up from the river, then we'll let them out.' Gary was already on the lookout for the roos.

'I know.' Mandy nodded, and they strolled on, through Dollar's field, where the goat and Art's few sheep munched at the short grass. The sheep saw them and came trotting up. They stared with their yellow eyes, then veered off as Dollar came down and demanded his treat.

'Whoa, steady!' Mandy laughed. Dollar almost pushed her over with his bony head. She fished in her pocket and found a mint. 'Here you are!' He nipped it from the palm of her hand, then he nudged again. 'No, that's all I've got, Dollar. Honestly!' She turned out her pockets to prove it.

He blew down his nose at her, then curled his lip to show off his long teeth. Then he tripped off down the hill to see who else he could pester.

'Quick!' Gary hopped over the wall into Moonbeam's field. 'Before he comes back and starts thinking he can eat *us*!'

Mandy scrambled after him. She gazed out across the compound. 'Wow, it's hot!' A heat-haze shimmered from the baked earth. She saw that the grass had dried out to a pale fawn. 'Where are the joeys? Can you see them?' The field seemed empty, except for bright blue butterflies and a grey-green lizard who basked on a nearby rock.

'Yep, under the tree!' Gary pointed to the shadiest spot, under a gum tree at the far edge of the compound.

The three joeys, dulled by the heat, had lain down to sleep. 'Best not wake them,' Mandy whispered. For a while they stood and watched the drowsy scene; pale grass, bright noisy insects, hot, hot sun.

'We need rain,' a quiet voice said. Art had followed them across Dollar's field and climbed over the wall to join them. 'If we don't get rain soon, a lot of farmers round here are gonna feel it bad.' He screwed up his face and squinted at the dense blue sky. Then he shrugged. 'Nope, not today.'

Gary kicked the toe of his shoe into the powdery earth. 'Did the others say when they were coming up?'

'No rush,' Art said. 'Anyhow, I thought you'd want to put off the goodbyes as long as you could.'

Gary didn't look up, but went on scuffing around in the dirt.

Mandy stepped in. 'I know what Gary means;

the longer we wait, the worse it gets.' She hated the build-up to saying goodbye. Once Moonbeam was safely off with the mob, she guessed they would all begin to feel better.

Art nodded. 'I reckon we're gonna miss little Moonbeam.'

'The worst bit will be not knowing how he's doing,' Gary admitted. It was the first time he'd let them know how he felt.

They watched the shadows lengthen under the gum tree. By now, the sun had thrown a red haze across the sky.

Art leaned against the wall. 'No worries there, mate,' he said. 'I'll be able to keep an eye on him every time the mob goes by. Ring me and ask me about him any time you want.'

'Or drop in?' Mandy suggested.

'Fine by me.' Art nodded. 'Right,' he said, snapping out of it. He stood up straight and dusted himself down. 'You can have a dollar apiece if you scoot back to the shack and bring a last armful of hay for the joeys!'

'No worries!' Gary made it clear that he thought this was easy money. He was already on his way. 'Get a move on, Mandy!'

'And tell your folks to come on up,' Art

reminded them. 'The mob will be coming by soon. They'll miss it if they don't watch out.'

They ran down the hill with the message, back through Dollar's field. In the yard, they found that the picnic had been cleared away.

'It looks like it's time.' Emily Hope stood and brushed crumbs from her trousers.

'Yes. You go straight up. We've got to fetch some hay,' Mandy said. She went to the shack, grabbed a bundle and gave it to Gary. Then she dug into the stack and took an armful for herself. They set off up the hill again, after the grown-ups.

'Er, one problem!' Gary balanced on the wall of Dollar's field. He looked down at Mandy, then up the field.

Mandy peered over the wall. Hooves thundered towards them. Dollar kicked up dust as he galloped down.

'Watch out!' Don Simpson yelled. The four grown-ups were caught mid-field. He whisked his wife out of the path of the eager goat.

Gary teetered on top of the wall. 'Dollar thinks the hay's for him!' As the goat careered closer, Gary lost his balance, wobbled, and chucked the armful of hay into the air as he tried desperately to save himself. It scattered and drifted to the ground. Gary landed in the field with a thump.

'Gary?' Mandy heard teeth chomping. She peered again. 'Are you OK?'

'Great!' he moaned. Dollar chomped and gobbled the scattered hay.

'Keep him busy!' she whispered. 'I'll sneak by with this second lot of hay!'

'Keep him busy yourself!' Gary stood up, dusting hayseed and dirt from his hair.

'Please!' Mandy hid the hay behind her back as she climbed the wall.

Muttering to himself, Gary grabbed a handful of hay and waved it under the goat's nose. He tempted Dollar away from the spot where Mandy would land. The goat took the bait. 'Go now!' Gary, whispered.

Mandy jumped and landed. She began to sprint up the hill. But Dollar wasn't about to be fooled.

'Get a move on, he spotted you!' Gary yelled.

'Run, Mandy!' Her dad stood halfway up the field, cheering her on as if it was a school sportsday.

Clutching the precious hay, Mandy sprinted

on. The goat's hot breath was on her neck. She reached the far wall and vaulted neatly over, then collapsed in a heap at the edge of the compound.

'You made it,' Art said. He took no notice of the hullaballoo in the field.

Mandy gasped and held out the hay. 'Here it is!'

'Good on you!' Art's face broke into a grin. 'Fancy old Dollar letting you get clean away. He must be slipping!' He fished a dollar from his pocket and handed it to her.

Mandy took it and glanced back at the wall. A row of faces grinned down at her; her mum and dad's, Gary's, Mr and Mrs Simpson's. And of course, Dollar's.

'You take the hay to the joeys,' Emily Hope suggested. 'We'll make our way round to that outcrop of rocks over there and watch for the mob. OK?'

So Art and Mandy were left to say a quiet goodbye to Moonbeam, Mitch and Star, who woke as the sun went down and came bounding lazily towards them, without a shadow of fear. They were three confident, strong young kangaroos, ready to test their skills in the outside world.

'Here you go!' Mandy shared the hay between the three of them. But she made a special fuss of Moonbeam; he was still her favourite. The memory of him, scared and alone on the road in the moonlight after his mother had been carried to their Landcruiser, would stay with her for a long time.

He took the hay from her in delicate handfuls, picking at it and pulling with his teeth. When Star came too close, he stuck out his chest and went up on his toes, warning him off. Mandy laughed.

'I reckon he'll do OK,' Art said. He looked pleased with himself. Together they tempted the joeys to the gate of the compound, ready to let them out to meet the mob.

Art waved to the Simpsons and Mandy's mum and dad, who had by now reached the lookout rock. 'Any sign?' he shouted.

'Yep. They're on their way!' Adam Hope replied.

Mandy swallowed hard as Art shot the bolt on the gate to the compound and let it swing wide. 'Go on, Moonbeam,' she whispered. She knew the other two joeys would follow him.

Moonbeam looked at the open gate, head to

one side. He hopped towards it, through it, and back into the compound.

He came close to Mandy and looked at her with his big, soft eyes. His long ears twitched as he cocked his head to one side.

'No, go on! It's time to go!' She herded him out again with her arms wide, whooshing him through the gate.

He looked out and tried again; a second bite at freedom. He hopped as far as the dark rocks, peered up and down the hill. Mitch and Star came after him; twitching, sniffing, exploring every little bit of ground.

'Here they come!' Adam Hope said again. 'The mob!' The sun had vanished behind the horizon, and all the colour drained from the valley as the herd of kangaroos made its way up the hill.

Satisfied that the three joeys were ready to go, Mandy and Art went to climb the rock. They joined the others in an eerie silence.

'Look!' Gary spotted the boss male in the herd cut off from the rest and leap ahead, tail thumping, ears cocked. Two other males followed at a distance.

He'd seen the joeys and they saw him. Plucky

Moonbeam stood fast. For a second it looked as if he would challenge the boss.

'Oh, no!' Mandy shut her eyes. Moonbeam wasn't ready to fight; he was too young, too inexperienced. The boss male would win hands down. When she opened her eyes again, she half-expected to see the two kangaroos locked in battle.

But Moonbeam had done the sensible thing for once. There he was crouching and coughing, as if saying, *Please let us join your mob.* Behind him, Mitch and Star did the same.

The boss hopped round them, head to one side. He strutted before them, showing his size, his strength. *Yes, you can join my mob as long as you don't think of challenging me just yet,* he seemed to say. He arched his back and showed his teeth, while Moonbeam, Mitch and Star kowtowed.

At last, the boss male nodded and admitted them to the mob. He bounded off up the hill, followed by three faithful new gang members.

Mandy breathed a sigh of relief. The whole herd moved on, fifty or sixty strong, ever on the lookout, alert to every sound, every scent, every movement in the dry scrub.

'It's weird!' Don Simpson gazed after them. 'I

could swear they were almost human!'

'Like women in old-fashioned long skirts!' Abbie Simpson agreed. 'It's eerie!'

'They're quite something,' he admitted. 'I reckon I never looked properly at a roo before!'

Mandy grinned at Gary. He stood next to her on the rock, smiling to himself.

'That's it. Well done!' Her mum said at last. Dusk gathered; now they could make out only the dark outline of the roos against the hillside.

'Time to get back home,' her dad said quietly.

Their group split up and went down in twos and threes to Art's yard.

'OK?' Mrs Hope asked, as they crossed the empty compound.

She nodded. 'If I'd been a joey like Moonbeam, I reckon I'd have wanted to join a mob and take my chances out there!' She turned and looked back. The roos had long vanished into the dusk. She felt proud of them all; Art, Gary, herself, and the three brave joeys in the big wide world.

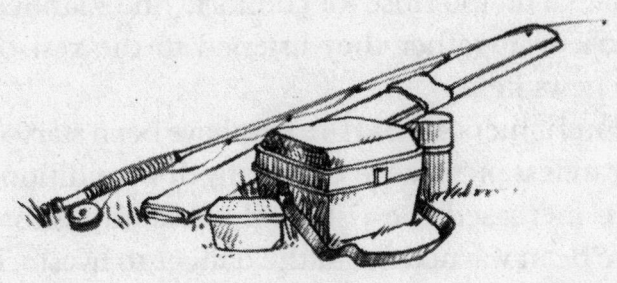

Eight

'The hot dry weather has brought a fire hazard
to many parts of New South Wales!' Mandy sat
in the family kitchen at Mitchell Gap and
watched the midday news. It was a few days after
their picnic, when they'd sent Moonbeam off
with the mob. The weather was scorching as
ever. 'The drought continues, and conditions
north of Sydney are said to have reached crisis
level.'

'Listen to this, Mum,' Mandy said, as the
newsreader reported a forest fire in the
mountains north of Eurabbie.

Emily Hope looked up from her newspaper.

'That's a bit too close for comfort.' She sounded worried. Together they listened to the rest of the news item.

'Firefighters say the fire may have been started by careless picnickers. Unusually dry conditions have increased the risk, and weekend visitors have been warned about the danger to livestock and wildlife in the region.'

The television screen showed film of the fire; a screen of billowing smoke, orange flames which laid waste to a whole hillside. Mandy watched, feeling helpless and scared.

'Don't worry; they'll soon have it under control,' her mum said. She turned off the television. 'And the weather forecast says it'll rain before too long. Once this dry spell ends, there's not so much danger of fire.'

Mandy nodded and wandered to the window. She was at a loose end, moping after Moonbeam and wondering how he was.

'What do you plan to do this afternoon?' Emily Hope reached for her white coat, ready to go back to work.

'Hmm? Oh, go to the beach, I expect.'

'Do you want a lift?' She glanced at her watch. 'Come on, I've got time. I'll take you over to

Waratarah. Is Gary going too?'

'Yep. He wants to practise for a competition this weekend.' Mandy stopped worrying about the forest fire – there was nothing she could do about it. Instead, she decided to set about enjoying the rest of the day. 'He's got a pretty good chance, he thinks.'

So she hopped into the car with her mum, and together they rode over to Gary's house, where, to her surprise, they found Art sitting on the patio, having lunch with Don and Abbie Simpson.

'Hi!' Mandy jumped out, pleased to see him. 'What are you doing here?'

'G'day.' He blushed as she noticed his smart pale blue shirt and new jeans. 'I've taken the day off,' he said.

'Yes, at last we persuaded him to take some time out and come and visit!' Abbie Simpson looked truly pleased. She drew Mandy to one side as Emily Hope gave a friendly wave and drove off. 'You know, if it hadn't been for you and that little orphan joey, Art would never have got round to inviting Don and me to that picnic!'

Mandy swallowed hard, hoping that Art

Simpson hadn't overheard. It was her turn to go red. 'It was Gary, really,' she protested. 'He was the one who took us to Munroah in the first place.'

'Well, anyway, thanks to you two, all that old fuss about money has been put to one side and Don and Art are beginning to see they have much more in common than they thought. Art came over on the early bus, and now they plan to go fishing for the afternoon. It's what they used to do when they were kids!'

She went inside to call Gary and tell him that Mandy had arrived. 'It'll do them both good,' she confided when she came back. 'Art spends far too much time by himself, tucked away at Munroah, and Don needs to take a break from work. And you know something? I heard Don telling his brother that he could see for the first time what Art sees in the wildlife round here. It's since we all saw the joeys from the lookout rock. Don's changed. He's even saying that work isn't the most important thing in the world any more!'

Mandy was glad that everyone was happy. While she waited for Gary to show up, she went and chatted to Art. 'Have you seen Moonbeam lately?' she asked straight off.

'Hah!' Don Simpson fished in his pocket and flipped a coin at his brother.

'What's that for?' she asked.

Art winked. 'We made a bet. I bet that was the first thing you'd say; "How's Moonbeam? Have you seen the joey?" '

She grinned. 'OK, so have you?' She didn't mind being teased like this.

'Yep, last night, up by the creek. Looking good, looking like he was part of the mob, no worries.' Art leaned back in his seat. 'I reckon he's getting into the swing of this living in the wild lark.'

'Did you see him this morning?'

'No. I was up before dawn to do the chores and catch the bus. No worries, though. The mob does the same thing, day in, day out. They come down from the ridge to graze. That's where they'll be now, down on the river flats.'

Mandy pictured Moonbeam spending the whole day grazing, a true member of the mob.

'You know, part of me's real proud of him,' Art went on. 'And part of me thinks, "Will he watch out for dingoes? Will he steer clear of the roads? Will he get in too many fights?" '

'Me too!' Mandy confessed. Sometimes she lay awake at night worrying.

'Just like me and Abbie over Gary!' Don laughed. 'When he's out on his surfboard. "Will he take a wave he can't handle? Will a rip pull him off-course?" '

Just then, Gary appeared from the house with two boards; one for Mandy, one for himself. 'No way!' he promised, cheerful as ever.

'No, I reckon you could ride one of those boards before you could walk!' Don chuckled proudly.

They loaded the car with the boards and the fishing gear, then the four of them set off for the beach. As they drove down the winding road into town, they made plans to meet up again at the end of the afternoon.

'I'll need to get back,' Art said. 'To check up on the animals back home. I can't leave them too long, or old Dollar will kick up a fuss.'

'Pity,' Don grumbled. 'We could have hired the boat for the whole evening as well.'

Mandy stole a look at Gary to see if she could guess what he was thinking. They were driving down the main street, past Merv Pyke's grocery store.

'Are you thinking the same as me?' Gary quizzed.

'Something about Dollar?'

'And the cats, and the sheep?' He nodded.

'Right!' They slapped palms, then leaned forward to suggest their idea to Art. '*We* could go up to Munroah and check the animals for you!' Mandy said. *And take a look at the joeys!* she thought.

'We could feed them, no worries,' Gary added.

Art half-turned in his seat. 'It's a good idea, thanks. But how would you get up there?'

It was the sight of Merv's shop that had given Mandy the possible answer to a problem she'd already thought of. 'We could try and get a lift with Merv. He goes past your place every day on his delivery round, doesn't he?'

'Wicked!' Gary jumped at this. 'Let's go and ask him now!'

Don Simpson put on the brake. They squealed to a halt. 'What do you think?' he asked his brother.

Art shrugged. 'It sounds like a whole lot of trouble.'

'Yes, but think of it; fishing right through the evening! Clear blue sea, no worries, knowing that everything's taken care of. And I could drive you up to your place after, and pick the kids up at the same time!' Don painted a picture that was hard to resist.

Still Art hesitated. 'What if Merv says no?'

'Let's go and ask!' Mandy was already out of the car, Gary at her side. 'I'm sure he won't mind.'

'OK, go ahead.' Art gave into the pressure, and they went ahead with their plan.

Inside the empty store, Mandy and Gary glanced along the aisles and behind the counter. 'Merv?' Gary called.

In the back of the shop, Merv's friendly greyhound, Herbie, barked. Soon Merv came through, a pencil tucked behind his ear. He carried a tray of bread for the shelves. When he spied Gary and Mandy, he grunted. 'Weather's breaking. Better get yourselves down to the beach if you want to get in some surfing before the rain comes.'

As it happened, there wasn't a cloud in the sky, Mandy knew. But she also knew better than to argue with Merv, who always thought the worst. 'OK, thanks. Actually, we wondered if we could grab a lift with you later on.'

'Where to?' He made a show of being busy. He placed the loaves in neat rows on the shelf.

'To Munroah, my uncle's place,' Gary told him. 'He's taken the day off, and we want to go up and keep an eye on things for him till he gets back.'

'Munroah?'

Somehow Merv made it sound like they'd asked him to take them to the moon. 'It wouldn't be out of your way, would it?' She stood waiting for the storekeeper's answer, knowing that he might invent a dozen reasons to say no.

'I do go that way, past Munroah,' he agreed. 'But I don't come back by the same road. I go straight on to Mitchell, and then down the other side in a full circle.'

'That's OK,' Gary said quickly. 'Dad will pick us up later!'

'I could be pretty loaded down,' Merv said glumly.

'We'll squeeze in!' Mandy promised.

There was a silence. 'You say you're helping Art out so he can take time off?' Time off wasn't something Merv approved of, obviously.

'To go fishing with Dad,' Gary added.

'Fishing?' This did it; it swung things round their way. 'Fishing's a great relaxation,' he told them. 'I'm a fishing man myself.' He went to the door of the store and looked out at the long curve of the bay. 'You'd better be here at five o'clock, OK? No later.' He turned to Gary. 'Tell your dad and uncle to have a good trip.' Then he went back to stacking his shelves.

Gary gave Mandy a thumbs-up sign. They raced back to the car with the good news.

'It's OK, you can go fishing for as long as you want!' Mandy told Art, while Gary lifted the boogie boards out of the back of the car. 'Don't worry; we'll look after everything for you!'

They were all set to go their separate ways; Art and Don Simpson to a small marina at one end of the bay where they would hire a fishing-boat, and Mandy and Gary to join the crowd on the beach.

Art leaned out of the car for a final word with Mandy. 'I reckon you'll take a look at the joeys while you're at it?' he said quietly.

She nodded happily. 'Yep, you bet!' It would be their special treat; to go up to the lookout rock and see Moonbeam with his mob.

'Say hello to them from me!' Art said with a nod.

'We sure will!'

They waved and went off to ride the surf.

Nine

All afternoon they surfed and lazed about. Mandy was determined to make the most of the sun and sea. Mostly she followed Gary's lead and chose the best waves at just the right moment. There was the thrill of watching the blue-green water rise and swell, the tingling moment when the first tiny ripples of white foam appeared on the crest of the wave. Then the surf broke. Mandy rode the crashing foam, caught on the big surge towards the white sands.

Just before five, she picked up her dripping board and trotted through the shallow water on to the beach for the last time. Gary was already waiting, his board slotted under one arm.

'Good one!' he grinned.

'Thanks.' She caught her breath. 'Ready?' It was time to make their way back to Merv's store.

'OK, come on.' He raced ahead.

'There's Herbie.' She spotted the greyhound, his thin, curved tail wagging. He stood at the roadside, by Merv's delivery-van, while the storekeeper himself carried bread, milk and eggs out from the shop.

'Here,' he said, abrupt as ever. He handed Mandy a box full of eggs. 'Put those in the back, and mind you don't break any.'

It was the first of many orders; 'Leave that here . . . put that there . . . mind you don't drop this,' delivered in a gruff voice by the middle-aged grumbler.

At last they were ready to set off, prepared to fetch and carry for Merv as he stopped off at houses and farms on the way to Munroah. He ticked things off with his pencil in a little red book as Mandy and Gary ran to the doors with the orders of bread, milk and eggs.

Then they were out of town, crawling along the twisting hill roads towards Art's place. Mandy kept a lookout, squashed in the middle beside Merv, with Gary on the far side, and Herbie perched comfortably in between them. By now the sun was low on the horizon, beginning to set over the distant blue mountains to the west. She noticed the wallabies and kangaroos picking their way slowly through the bush.

'Look, they're already heading up on to the ridge,' she said. She pointed out a small mob by the roadside.

'No worries, we're nearly there.' Gary leaned out of the window. 'Yep. Could you drop us here, please?' he asked Merv, who pulled up by the creaking old sign.

Merv pulled up and they jumped out. 'Thanks a lot!' Mandy cried, eager to get on.

Merv gave a small nod. Herbie poked his head out of the window and barked. 'Watch out for the storm,' Merv warned. 'It could hit any time. And make sure that goat is safe in the shack. He won't like thunder!'

She took a deep breath. 'OK, Merv, thanks!' At this rate they would miss the roos.

'And here – don't forget Art's order!'

Mandy and Gary were so eager to see the joeys that they'd forgotten Art's groceries. They waved

and ran down the rough track towards the smallholding, while Merv's white van pulled slowly away.

'What thunderstorm?' she asked. The sky was clear; not a cloud in sight, though a wind had got up, she noticed. It rustled through the dry grass like waves on the sea.

'Never mind him,' Gary told her. 'You know what Merv's like.'

Soon Art's battered caravan came into view, almost smothered by creepers. Grass sprouted from under the floor, into every nook and cranny. The yard was scattered with wild flowers. Bees hummed, heavy with pollen.

'There's Ed.' Mandy spotted him on the top step. Then Al slunk out from under the caravan, miaowing as they arrived. Both cats came to weave themselves between their bare legs.

Mandy stooped to stroke Ed. 'Poor things, they're hungry!' He purred and pushed his nose against her hand.

They fed the cats with food stored in one of the shacks, then they went to find Dollar in his field. Mandy took a good armful of hay to tempt him back to the shack for the night.

'G'day, Dollar!' Gary climbed the wall to his field and sat astride it.

The goat ignored him and made a beeline for Mandy. She laughed. 'Here comes food!' He snatched at the hay, rolled his tongue round a big clump and shoved it into his mouth. Soon he was munching noisily. 'Poor old thing, you've been by yourself all day!' Mandy chatted softly, letting him go ahead with eating his supper. 'I bet you haven't seen a soul for hours!'

He shook another mouthful of hay from the bundle which she held out. Back went his head, as he blew through his nostrils.

Mandy used the hay to lead him towards the

gate. When they got there, Gary held it open for the goat to trot through, while Mandy backed off towards the yard. Dollar followed, good as gold, nibbling at the hay as they went. Before he knew it, Mandy had led him into his shack and cornered him there.

'Good boy, you stay here nice and safe,' she cooed at him. He stamped his foot. 'Now, there's no use being cross. I got you here fair and square, and here you've got to stay!' Quickly she drew the door closed. Dollar brayed and stamped.

'He's not happy,' Gary laughed.

'No, but Merv might be right, you never know. If it rains, goats hate the wet. He's much better inside here, just in case.' Mandy made sure the old door was firmly bolted.

Now she was keen to head on back through the field and across the joeys' old compound towards the roo track. She realised how late it was; the sun had sunk behind the hill and the whole valley was in shadow. 'Do you think we've missed them?' she asked as they went.

'No worries,' Gary said.

But they broke into a run, heading for the big, dark rocks; their lookout point for the kangaroos. When they got there, they scrambled to the top and gazed down the valley, hoping for a sign that the mob was on its way.

Mandy searched the long slope, across a stretch of empty scrub. She felt the wind tug at her clothes, saw that clouds had gathered in the east.

Gary saw it too. 'That could be rain on its way,' he told her. 'If Merv's right about the storm, I hope Dad and Uncle Art have kept an eye on things. They'd have problems out in a boat if a storm hits.'

'They'll be OK,' Mandy said. 'They know what they're doing.' But she was uneasy now, still scanning the slope for the kangaroos. She noticed that Art's sheep, which today wandered free in the hills above the farm, were coming down closer to home. And there were rabbits everywhere. They bobbed across the scrub and vanished with a flash of white tail into burrows dug into the dry earth. Normally the rabbits would stay out at dusk, to groom and graze. And there was another odd thing; in the tall eurabbie trees higher up the hill, a kookaburra began a screeching cry that set her nerves on edge.

'Come on, roos, where are you?' Gary crept

to the very edge of the rock and peered down the valley. 'You don't think they've taken a new track, do you?' he asked.

'No, Art says they always come this way!' They waited, watching for any sign.

And then, one by one they came. They bounded out of the valley across the scrub towards the rock. The big male came first, checking the lie of the land, followed by two other adult males and a huddle of females, with joeys safely in their pouches.

Mandy breathed a sigh of relief. She recognised the boss male and his deputies. Soon Moonbeam would appear, with Mitch and Star. 'I don't think they like this wind.' She watched the leading roos stop to twitch their heads this way and that. Tonight there was no stopping to groom and scratch; there seemed to be an extra watchfulness, almost a fear among them.

'No, I reckon the wind makes it hard for them to smell their way along,' Gary said.

'And it cuts out all the little sounds they go by, as well.' Like dingoes creeping through the undergrowth, making a twig crack, a bush rustle. By now, the wind was rushing through the grass and the trees.

'There's Moonbeam!' Gary spotted him, flanked by Mitch and Star. The trio bounded up the hill together. Moonbeam's white chest was puffed out proudly as he led the way, ears pricked, tail thumping.

'Hi, Moonbeam!' Mandy waved and called.

He heard her voice and veered off-course towards the lookout rock, cutting away from the other two joeys. Quickly they scrambled down to join him.

'You haven't forgotten us, then!' Mandy ran to him. He was just the same, with his lovely, long face and big, dark eyes, his cheeky look. Yet she thought he was taller, faster after his few days of freedom.

The rest of the mob ran on, streaming out of the valley past the rock, moving on as if unsettled by the wind. For a minute or two, Mandy stroked Moonbeam's ears and nose, talking gently. Then she sighed and stood back. 'Go on, you'd better hurry and catch them up.'

Moonbeam swivelled his long ears, twitched his nose. Strange scents were in the air, carried by the wind. Gusts rushed up the hill, into the trees above the farm. He gave a grunt and tossed his head.

'Go on!' she urged. The boss male was already across the clearing and out of sight.

But a new sound rose above the wind; the man-made sound of a car engine that disturbed the stragglers at the back of the mob and made Moonbeam roll his eyes in fear.

'There!' Gary pointed high up the hill to where a Landcruiser rocked and roared out of the gum trees. It dipped across the rough territory, into a creek, up the bank, heading across country. Its headlights shone in the gloom, and as it passed close to their lookout rock, they could see a family inside; mother, father, and three children in the back, all loaded up with tents and camping gear.

'Go on, Moonbeam!' Mandy stood between the frightened animal and the car. It was a safe distance away, but the joey was terrified. All he knew was that cars were bad. 'This one won't harm you. Go on, quick!'

At last he broke out of his frozen fear. He leaped away from the sound and glare of the car, bounding for all he was worth after the mob.

Gary and Mandy watched him safely out of sight. He caught up with the stragglers; a small joey and its mother, then Star. Soon they all entered the shadow of the trees.

'Funny, they were pretty edgy even before that Landcruiser showed up.' Gary frowned down the hill as they turned to watch it disappear.

'Some people!' Mandy concentrated on the camping family. In their race across country they'd managed to spoil the reunion with Moonbeam.

She shrugged, and they set off from the lookout rock towards Art's farm, planning one last check on the animals. Her thoughts turned towards keeping them safe from the storm that was blowing in.

But then, as the winds blew and the clouds gathered, the whole world seemed to turn upside down. The roos, who had vanished into the trees high on the hill, suddenly came leaping back. They bounded from between the eurabbies out into the scrub. They scattered in all directions, gathering speed and calling out in the dusk. Mothers leaped through the bush with their joeys, the males ran ahead. The whole mob split up, seized by panic.

'What is it, what's wrong?' Mandy's heart was in her mouth. This was more than wind and storm clouds; something more dreadful was taking place. She ran back towards the rock, with Gary alongside. Together they scrambled up the rough slope, scraping their knees and shins, trying to see what it was that had panicked the kangaroos.

'It's something in those trees!' Gary gasped. He flung an arm in their direction.

'What?' Mandy swung round, confused. 'Where's Moonbeam? Have you seen him?' She'd spotted Mitch, fleeing alone into the valley. 'Gary, the wind's changed direction! What's happening?'

It swept around the rock, coming at them from this way and that. It gathered force, sweeping down the hillside from the west, flattening the sea of dry grass under it.

'Wait a minute! The storm should be brewing up from the sea. But whatever spooked the roos is up on the ridge!' He looked on helplessly as the kangaroos leaped in crazy, zigzagging tracks across the scrub.

'Here's Moonbeam!' Mandy cried out in relief.

He came charging out of the trees. Star was with him. But when Star picked up speed to follow the leaders into the valley, Moonbeam made straight for the lookout rock.

'We're here!' Mandy stood and waved both arms. 'He's looking for us!'

He charged at the steep rock and took it in two bounds. Mandy and Gary stepped back. Moonbeam poised, turned, then took a mighty leap back to the ground. He looked up at them, watching, waiting for them to follow.

'What is it, Moonbeam?' In the gathering gloom, against the roar of the wind, Mandy's voice sounded small and frightened.

Again he bounded on to the rock. His nostrils quivered in terror.

Mandy tried to imagine what this was; this great fear that had sent the kangaroos fleeing down the hill. She knew Moonbeam had come to warn them. 'What is it? What is it?' Her own senses grew sharp with the same fear. She looked and she sniffed . . . Smoke!

It wound its way into her nostrils, a thin stream of danger. Once smelled, it caught in her throat; a dry, hot, clinging smoke, slightly sweet, like burning grass, like bushfire, forest fire. The smell of disaster.

'Fire!' she cried.

Moonbeam's tail thumped the rock. He leaped to the ground. He was warning them, wanting them to escape with the rest of the mob. He sat poised, waiting to see if they would follow.

'Over there!' Gary stood on the peak of the rock and pointed towards the trees.

Mandy saw a flicker of orange, and now a cloud of smoke billowing down the hill towards them. So this was why the campers in the Landcruiser had fled! Fire in tinder-dry trees. Flames that would trap them if the wind turned and swung in from the west.

'It's heading this way!' she yelled at Gary. 'The wind's fanning the flames towards us!' She was gripped with a fear that froze her to the spot and squeezed in a tight band round her chest.

'The farm!' he cried.

'The animals!' There was no one to help. Munroah was deserted; it was up to them.

The orange glow spread through the trees. They could hear the flames catch and roar.

They had to run to get Dollar out of his shack before the flames swept down the hill. They must save whoever they could!

Ten

'Moonbeam, run!' Mandy cried. The fire roared through the trees. She scrambled down from the lookout rock through thickening smoke.

But the joey refused to flee with the rest of the mob. He stuck by her side, fear flickering in his eyes. His nostrils flared in terror.

'Come on, Mandy!' Gary leaped to the ground. His hoarse voice drifted on the wind. Then he sprinted, head down, across the scrub towards the farm.

For a moment, panic seized her whole body. What if the swirling wind swept downhill faster than they could run? How would they escape the flames? She saw that the hillside was alive with terrified wildlife. A mob of wallabies came screeching out of the forest, past the lookout rock, tumbling and rolling in their flight. They crashed by on either side. Slower, smaller creatures hurried through the grey smoke; spiny echidnas shuffling through the scrub on their short legs, snouting for shelter, then scurrying on in another cloud of smoke. Emus ran by, awkward on their stilt-legs, and the ground teemed with rabbits bolting ahead of the flames.

'Mandy!' Gary stopped at the compound gate and called again.

She could still see him through the smoke and gloom. Another tree flared at the deadly touch of the yellow flames. The fire raged on, high into the dusk sky.

Mandy knew she must act. She turned to Moonbeam. 'Go!' she pleaded.

He stood, blind with panic, his nose filled with the terrible smell of burning.

'You can't come with me, you have to go down to the river. Wait there for us!' She grew desperate as Moonbeam still refused to leave her side. She began to run towards Gary, stopped and tried to shoo the joey away. He

stuck with her; his only guide and protector.

'Mandy, the fire's heading straight for Munroah!' Gary cried. His voice was almost drowned in the crackling flames. 'I'm going to see if I can get Dollar out!'

She lost him in a sudden whirl of smoke. Pulled between him and Moonbeam, she began to run through the bush. She stumbled, caught her leg in a spiky bush, twisted her ankle and fell. Her eyes smarted with pain and smoke, but she felt Moonbeam bending over her, waiting for her to get up and run again. She pushed herself on to her knees, then stood up, testing her weight on the injured ankle. There was a new rush of animals coming towards her in a burst of terrified screeches and howls.

'Go! Go with them!' Mandy pleaded with the joey again. If he didn't flee now with all the rest, it would be too late.

Then, out of a haze of drifting smoke, as the wind gusted round in a new direction, two more roos appeared. They bounded full-speed into the valley, crashing through all obstacles. But they saw Moonbeam, lost and cut off from his mob. They swerved across the hillside to collect him.

'Mitch! Star!' Mandy recognised the two half-grown joeys.

Moonbeam shot round at the sound of their thumping tails, to see their strong young bodies hurtling through the bush. He took one leap towards them, turned and looked at Mandy.

'Yes, go!' She herded him towards his mates, begging him to save himself.

And his instinct for the herd took over. He wanted to be with them, part of the fleeing mob. As Mitch and Star came to take him with them, one on either side, Moonbeam saw what he must do to survive. His head went up, he crouched on his enormous back legs and took off. He was away with his friends, pounding over the ground away from Mandy, away from the flames to the safety of the river flats.

Mandy half-sobbed and turned away. Now she must run to the farm. Pain shot through her ankle, but she pressed on, through the compound, over the wall into Dollar's field, feeling the heat of the fire in the smoky air. She must catch up with Gary, who had run ahead, out of sight.

She ran and clambered on to another wall into Art's overgrown yard. But as she paused on top and glanced back, she heard movements behind her. There were creatures trapped in the field. What were they? She peered through the smoke, and as it thinned, she made them out; Art's sheep!

They blundered against one another, stumbled towards the wall, and set up a pathetic bleating as they realised that Mandy was their only hope of escape.

So she had to stop again, desperate now to find Gary and help him with Dollar and the cats. The smoke grew thicker again, the air hotter, and she could feel the glow of the flames on her face. They were still hundreds of metres up the hill, but growing fiercer, more out of control.

She jumped back down into the field, deciding to try and head the huddle of sheep towards the gate that led into Art's yard. She shouted and waved her arms, ducking low to dodge the worst of the smoke. Her plan was to keep the sheep ahead of her in a tight group, but they skittered and bumped, their hooves raised dust, their eyes rolled with fear. It took precious time to get them in the corner of the field, trapped together beside the closed gate.

And now she was stuck. How could she wade through the sheep to open the gate, without leaving them to scatter? If she left them for a second, they would veer off in all directions and head back into the smoke. All her effort would be lost. She raised her voice. 'Gary, come quick!' Would he hear? Would he find them in the gloom?

He did; he came running at her call. He appeared from the yard, his face streaked with sweat and dirt, his T-shirt ripped.

'Open the gate, let them out!' Mandy struggled to keep the sheep together. One tried to bolt. She stood in its path and shooed it back into the huddle.

Quick to see what was needed, Gary flung open the gate and let them through. The sheep barged into everything in their rush to escape. They brought the gate off its hinges, charged at Gary, turned and made for the open yard.

'If we get them on to the track up to the road, they can keep running!' he yelled over the sound of their trampling hooves. He coughed as smoke caught in his throat. 'Once they're up there, they'll find their own way down into the valley!'

Mandy came up from behind. She collected

stragglers, urged them on. At last, the sheep
were through the yard, running between the
fences of Art's driveway, on to the road ahead.

Gary gasped and doubled over to catch his
breath.

'You OK?' Her ankle throbbed, she felt the
sweat run through her hair, down her face and
neck.

He nodded. 'Where's Moonbeam?'

'With the mob. Mitch and Star came to fetch
him!'

'Good!'

'How about Dollar?'

'Still in the shack. But I can't find the cats!'
He stood upright, heaving air into his lungs.

Behind them, a wall of fire swept the hillside.
Fingers of flame crept from the forest down
the scrub, setting light to the long, dry grass,
leaping and jumping in spurts of orange, yellow
and red. In no time, the fire would reach the
lookout rock, then the tinder-dry compound,
the field and the farm!

For a second Mandy closed her eyes tightly.
But the roar and crackle of the flames seemed
to grow louder. The unkind wind still swept
down the hill, driving a blast of heat against

her face. She opened her eyes. 'Where did you try looking for the cats?'

Gary set off running back across the yard towards the shack. 'In the caravan. They're not there.'

'No, Art usually lets them roam free. I can't see a thing!' She raised an arm to shield her eyes.

'Let's get Dollar out first, then worry about the cats!' He reached the door of the shack and wrenched at the bolt. They could hear Dollar's hooves clatter against the wooden walls, and the thin sound of a goat whinnying in terror.

Mandy stood back while Gary shoved the bolt free. The shack was flimsy and unsafe in the face of the wind; the open window banged, the door creaked on its hinge.

'It's OK, Dollar, we've come to get you!' She stepped inside, into the dark stall where poor Dollar stood tethered.

Panic-stricken by the noise, the glare and the smoke, the goat pulled at his tether. He kicked out at the wooden partition which kept him penned into his sleeping-quarters.

'Watch out!' Gary warned from outside the shack. 'He'll catch you with his hooves!'

She jumped aside. The hooves missed by centimetres. Growing more alarmed by the moment, still she tried to keep her voice calm as she reached for the knot which tied Dollar's rope to an iron ring on the wall. 'There, Dollar, don't pull. Stand still, there's a good boy.' Her fingers fumbled with the thick rope. Dollar had pulled the knot tight in his struggle to get free. 'I can't do it!' she gasped. The shack was filling with smoke, Dollar strained and pulled, the knot stuck fast. 'What shall we do now?'

'Steady, boy!' Gary felt his way into the shack to help. 'OK,' he decided. 'We have to all pull together!' He pointed to the iron ring on the shack wall to show Mandy that the wood had begun to splinter and split. 'With three of us tugging, I reckon that wood will shatter, then we can get Dollar out of here!'

She coughed, then held her breath, trying not to gulp in the sharp smoke. She nodded her head. 'Let's try!' She seized the rope close to the ring, while Gary grabbed it from behind. 'Pull!' she cried. They strained at the rope. 'Go on, boy, pull!'

Dollar seemed to realise what they were trying to do. He began to tug with his full weight. The

wooden board creaked and cracked, and the ring came free with a shattering wrench as the old wood finally gave way.

'Right, let's go!' Gary cried. His chest heaved with the effort of pulling Dollar free.

Dizzy, Mandy turned the goat round in his tiny stall. She led him into the yard. The ground swam beneath her feet and she walked unsteadily on her painful ankle. Yet she knew she had to keep on going through the smoke; anywhere, it didn't matter where, so long as it was away from the terrible fire.

Crazed by the blaze, his common sense gone,

Dollar reared up and jerked at the rope. Up and down he reared and clattered while Mandy held on grimly. She felt the rope slip and burn her hands, but she refused to let go.

'Hang on!' Gary came out of the shack. He dodged Dollar's flailing hooves. 'Don't let go of him, Mandy! We've got to get him out of here!'

By now the smoke was so thick and stinging, the air so hot that it was impossible to see which way to go. But through it all, through Dollar's whinnying and kicking, through the wind and the roaring flames, they picked up a new sound. It was a small, high cry; then two. Two more creatures calling for help.

'The cats!' Gary realised with a shock that Ed and Al were still lost somewhere in the yard. They mewed, high and terrified, as Mandy hung on to Dollar's rope, while the goat bucked and kicked and tried to pull free.

'Try under the caravan!' Mandy thought the sound came from low down and behind them. 'But don't be long. We've got to find the track and get Dollar on to the road!'

Gary ducked down and felt his way back to Art's van. At last, still unable to see, he stumbled against the metal steps. They clattered and tipped; the cats' howls grew louder. He heard them and dropped to his knees. 'Yep, they're under here!' he called.

'Quick, Gary!' She knew she couldn't hang on to Dollar for much longer.

He reached under the caravan, parting the overgrown grass and scrabbling with his fingertips. 'I can't feel anything!' He could hear them, but they were out of reach, crouching there too frightened to come out.

And just when Mandy knew she couldn't hold on to the goat a moment longer; when she would have to let him go and Gary would have to give up the search for Ed and Al, and the smoke would overpower them, the wail of a siren split the air. Two tones, long-short, repeated over and over, blaring nearer.

Gary staggered to his feet, blinded by smoke.

'Fire-engine!' Mandy cried. 'Come on, it's the fire-engine!' She let Dollar pull her towards the sound.

Blue lights flashed, the red engine roared down the track, headlights cutting through the smoke into the yard. Men jumped from the cab and ran towards them. Someone grabbed Dollar's rope, everything whirled and roared;

lights, engine, faces, voices, smoke, flames.
Mandy sank to the ground.

Eleven

When she came round, the fire-fighters had snaked their hoses across the yard and great fountains of water were drenching Art's caravan and shacks. They showered into the air and fell on the ground, driving back the smoke, splashing everything in sight.

'The cats?' Mandy mumbled. Her mouth was dry, her voice cracked. It was the first thing she thought of.

'It's OK,' a fire-fighter told her. 'One of our men is fetching them now. And we've got the goat up on the road. He's safe, don't worry.'

She nodded and tried to sit up. She found

she was propped against the fence in Art's driveway, out of the way of the spraying hoses. They'd wrapped a blanket round her shoulders. Gary crouched beside her, his hands clasped round his knees.

'Can they save the farm?' she whispered.

Men shouted, ran, pointed. They redirected a hose. Its powerful spray drenched the shacks. On the hill, the forest fire still burned.

'They're soaking everything, trying their best,' Gary assured her. 'They've got three more engines up there.' He pointed up the hill, and his face caught the glow of flames. It looked taut and exhausted.

She turned to the fireman who'd caught her when she collapsed. 'Will the farm burn down?' she insisted.

He shook his head. 'We're doing everything we can, but the wind's bad. It's in the wrong direction. If it goes on like this, I'm not sure!'

Smoke still billowed towards them, though the water from the hoses had cleared the air in the yard. There was noise and action all around. But the flames had a strong hold in the trees, on the scrub. They crept greedily close to Art's grazing-land. Within minutes, it seemed, his farm, his whole life could be swallowed up.

Then another helmeted figure came running through the spray. He held the two scared cats, one under each arm. Their black fur was soaked through; they were skinny as skeletons and they trembled from head to toe. But they were safe. The man handed them to Mandy, then ran back to join his team.

Carefully she slipped the blanket from her shoulders and used it to dry the shivering cats. Ed and Al whimpered and mewed. Gary helped to rub them dry as gently as he could, wrapping Ed up safe and sound inside the coarse woollen cloth.

'At least we saved Art's animals,' Mandy murmured. They were safe, every single one. Even if he did lose his farm, maybe he could take his sheep, his goat, his cats and start again. She stroked Al, then looked up as a car rushed down the track. More sirens blared, more people shouted and yelled instructions.

Footsteps ran towards them. 'Come this way!' A woman approached, wanting to lead them to a waiting ambulance.

Shakily Mandy got to her feet. 'We're OK,' she protested.

'No, you can't do anything else here,' the paramedic insisted quietly. She was kind and efficient; a young woman with a pretty face and curly dark hair. 'We have to get you out, just in case!'

They knew she was right, but still they hesitated, as if by being there they could stop the flames from engulfing Art's little farm. 'Can't we stay?' Gary asked.

The paramedic shook her head. 'Come on, we have to see if we can contact your parents. They must be worried sick about you.' She led them towards the ambulance, as fire-fighters shouted for more water.

Mandy's legs felt heavy as lead. Slowly she followed the young woman. Her head was still fuzzy, her eyes pricking in the smoky heat. The flashing blue lights made everything strange. For a moment she felt she might faint once more. She had to tilt her head to the sky to catch her balance and her breath. She held her face towards the burning hill and felt a cold drop against her cheek, then another and another. 'Rain!' She opened her mouth to utter the word. A drop fell on her tongue. They fell out of nowhere, out of the dark clouds that the smoke had hidden.

'It is, it's rain!' Gary spread his arms and yelled at the top of his voice. He whirled round. 'Oh wicked, it's raining!'

Mandy closed her eyes. She felt the rain begin to fall. It came down, slowly at first in great drops against her face, then harder, until it drenched her parched skin, her hair, her clothes. It washed away the smell of smoke, ran coolly down her body and soaked into the thirsty earth.

'There!' The paramedic took both her hands and spoke soothingly. 'Just in time.' Now she didn't need to hurry Mandy into the safety of the waiting ambulance.

The rain had arrived to quench the fire. It was a buster; a real, lashing, drenching storm, carried by the winds off the Pacific Ocean.

On the hillside above Eurabbie, the flames hissed and died under the downpour. They would flare again, then hiss and die into the night. Even a forest fire couldn't stand up to a summer storm.

Art's farm would be saved from destruction; his tiny paradise would survive.

By midnight they had all gathered at Mitchell

Gap to celebrate the escape from the fire; the Hopes, the Simpsons and Art. Art's sheep were rounded up by neighbours and kept safe in the run at the back of the surgery. Ed and Al were snug in baskets inside the kennels, and Dollar kept up a loud braying from the yard.

Don Simpson explained how their fishing trip had ended. 'We knew there was a storm brewing, we were out in the boat when it began to blow across, so we headed back to the marina double-quick.'

They sat in a cool breeze out on the veranda, drinking coffee and talking quietly. The rain, which had lasted for two hours, had left a blackened expanse where the fire had been. Now all was quiet, except for the slow drip as last drops fell from the trees round the Hopes' yard.

'And the first we heard of the fire was when a family drove off the hill into town. They set up the alarm.' Adam Hope gave their side of the story. 'They said they'd seen smoke and they drove down as fast as they could. They hadn't a clue what to do to stop it.'

Gary nodded. 'We saw them.' That would have been the car charging down the hill, stuffed full of camping gear.

'Well, they just piled everything and everyone into the car and drove like mad into Eurabbie. We've got them to thank for calling the fire-fighters.'

They talked it through; how they first realised that Mandy and Gary might be trapped at Munroah, the frantic telephone calls, the race up the hill towards the fire as the rain began to fall.

'When we got there, it was all over,' Mr Hope said. He sat back to sip his coffee. 'And of course, you were all safe, including the animals!'

'Thank heavens!' Abbie Simpson voiced what they all felt.

'I never thought I'd be so glad to see a buster!' Don Simpson put in. 'Even if it did put a sudden stop to our fishing trip!' He'd recovered his easy-going manner, though he swore the fire had frightened him half to death.

Mandy sat and listened, resting her foot on a stool. She noticed that Art had been quiet through all the relieved talk. Everyone was counting their blessings except him. Now she saw him get up and wander into the yard. She followed awkwardly, keeping the weight off her sprained ankle.

Art sauntered to the pool, then went to take a look up the quiet hill at the creek behind the house. She walked with him, pointing out the roots of the old acacia tree where a family of platypuses lived. He nodded and wandered on.

'Thanks,' he said at last. Just one word. They'd called in on Ed and Al, who purred at them from their baskets; soot-black, warm and dry. And now they stopped to talk to Dollar.

Mandy knew that what she and Gary had done to save Art's animals meant the world to him. She smiled shyly back. 'Anyone would have done the same,' she said.

'You could've run,' he pointed out. He stood with his hands in his pockets, staring up at the stars. 'Like that family in the car.'

She stopped a moment to think. 'No,' she said; 'we could never have done that. We had to think of the animals first, didn't we?'

They decided that it was best to wait until morning to take Art and his animals back to Munroah.

Merv Pyke had heard about Munroah's narrow escape. Straight away he volunteered to ring round his farmer friends to borrow a truck for the sheep. He turned up before breakfast towing a covered trailer on the back of his van. He gave orders to lower the ramp, and soon the sheep were loaded and on their way.

'Thanks, Merv!' Art waved him off on to the road.

'No worries!' he called back.

'Was that Merv I saw?' Mandy's mum came to the door.

Mandy nodded. 'Yes, but you might not have recognised him.'

'Why not?'

'He was smiling, that's why!'

They laughed.

Emily Hope insisted on driving Art back home. She said Dollar could go in the back of the Landcruiser, and the cats in the front, with Art, Gary and Mandy.

Embarrassed at all the trouble he thought he'd caused, Art accepted the lift.

So they set off soon after Merv had left with the sheep, taking their time, enjoying the fresh air that the buster had left in its wake.

Soon they reached the dip in the road by Art's farm. Emily Hope pulled up to get a view of the burnt hilltop. 'See, the fire didn't do too much damage,' she pointed out.

The ridge was scorched along a two hundred metre stretch. The patch of burnt earth went down the hill towards the sheltered hollow where the caravan nestled, but stopped short of their lookout rock. In the morning light it looked wrecked and sad; trees were blackened stumps, the earth ashen.

Quietly they moved on down Art's track.

'Those gum trees, they can come through a fire.' Art spoke up for the first time since they'd left Mitchell Gap.

'How come?' Mandy was puzzled. 'Are you saying they can grow again?'

'Yep.' He opened his door as Mrs Hope pulled up in the yard. Then he stepped out and stretched. He took a deep breath. 'Eucalyptus; it can survive drought and fire. Before too long, there'll be new leaves on those burnt branches.'

And the grass will grow again, and the birds and animals will come back, Mandy thought. *The rabbits, the echidna, the wallabies and the kangaroos.*

The morning air was calm and fresh, the

ground underfoot still damp, as she and Gary decided to walk up the hill to their lookout rock.

She climbed it slowly, eager to see signs that the valley would come back to life after its narrow escape. Already, little wallabies ran across the old roo track and magpies flew overhead. And to her delight, Mandy found they were in time to see a morning mist rise from the creek, drawn up by the warm sun. Beneath the mist she made out a herd of kangaroos; the Munroah mob, *their* mob. They settled to graze after the fire and storm of the night before. Life went on.

'There's Mitch,' Gary said quietly. 'And Star.'

The roos turned their heads at the sound of his voice, then went back to their grazing.

'And Moonbeam.' Mandy picked him out close to the rock. When he saw them, he reared up, thrust out his chest and strutted; the Moonbeam of old.

Mandy smiled, remembering the shivering orphan at the roadside. 'Watch out for kangaroos!' she whispered, remembering the warning notice.

'What?' Gary asked, keeping his eyes on the mob.

She paused. They smiled at each other and began to head back to Munroah to help Merv unload Art's sheep into the field. 'Nothing,' she said. 'I'm glad, that's all!'